About the autho

Nigel Hill

Nigel founder of The Leadership Factor, a company that specialises in helping organisations to measure, monitor and improve their customers' experience. With offices in the USA, Australia, Russia, Spain, Portugal and France as well as the UK, The Leadership Factor provides research services, advice and training worldwide. Nigel has written three previous books and many articles about customers and speaks at conferences and events around the world. He has helped organisations such as Manchester United FC, Chelsea FC, the BBC, ASDA, and Land Securities amongst many others.

Greg Roche

Client Director at The Leadership Factor. Greg is one of the UK's leading experts in helping organisations to use data from customer satisfaction surveys to improve their customer experience. He has worked with many different organisations across all sectors of the economy including Royal Bank of Scotland, Visa, Tarmac, Irish Life, Allied Irish Bank, Churchill, Privilege, Jurys Doyle Hotels, Sainsbury's Convenience and The Bank of New York.

Rachel Allen

Rachel is Client Manager at The Leadership Factor. She is an expert on customer satisfaction research and complaint handling. Rachel has written many articles and speaks widely on these subjects at conferences, seminars and other events. She works with many different organisations on surveys and complaint handling including Direct Line, Tesco, Royal Borough of Kensington and Chelsea, HBOS, Forensic Science Service and Royal Bank of Scotland International.

If you would like to contact any of the authors go to **www.customersatisfactionbook.com** and follow the contact instructions.

Acknowledgements

Many people have helped in the preparation of this book. Particular thanks to Robert Crawford, Director of the Institute of Customer Service for writing the Preface and for being a continual source of honest advice, stimulating views and professional support. Thanks also to the many clients and contacts from companies and organisations across all sectors of the economy who have helped to develop our ideas and understanding whilst grappling with their real work of improving customer satisfaction. Amongst these, very special thanks to those who reviewed this book, including Tim Oakes from the RBS, Mark Adams from Virgin Mobile, Scott Davidson from Tesco Personal Finance and Quintin Hunte from Fiat. All made many useful suggestions for amendments or additions. Needless to say any opinions, omissions or mistakes in the book are the responsibility of the authors.

There is much more to publishing a book than writing the words. Ask Rob Ward who not only did the typesetting and produced the diagrams but also had to amend it all, many times, as the authors had second, third, fourth thoughts and more. Thanks also to Ruth Colleton who cross-checked every single reference on the internet and, along with Janet Hill, corrected the proofs. Thanks to Rob Ward and Rob Egan for the cover design and to Charlotte and Lucy at Cogent Publishing for organising the never ending list of tasks that turn a manuscript into a printed book that you can buy in shops or on the internet!

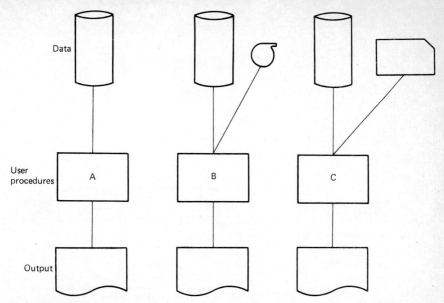

Fig. 10.1 Traditional application-oriented data processing

To implement this view, control of the physical storage of the data is entrusted to a data base management system (DBMS), and all applications to use the data must be passed through this system (Fig. 10.2). The DBMS is a set of software routines, and later in this chapter we shall discuss some ways in which a suitable system can be set up.

It is important to understand that nothing in a data base approach prevents each department from having responsibility for maintaining the accuracy of certain aspects of the data. This simply represents the devolution of authority for the data from the organisation as a whole to one of its subunits. In practice, **all** the data will be allocated to the responsibility of one department or another. The distinction is that only one department may now be chosen for any one item of data, and even this department will have to access its data through the medium of the DBMS.

Another misconception is that a data base never contains duplicated data. Although one of the objects in adopting a data base method of processing is to reduce unnecessary duplication there are some occasions when it is essential if reasonable processing efficiency is to be maintained. In such cases it should be part of the responsibility of the DBMS to ensure that the multiple copies remain compatible with each other and with their related data areas.

10.3 Data analysis

To establish genuine data independence when a data base is created (i.e. independence of the data from any one application where it is used) the first step in the implementation should be a thorough analysis of the data resources of the organisation. This should include the identification of the data which is used, where it originates and why it is needed, the reconciliation of differences in terminology

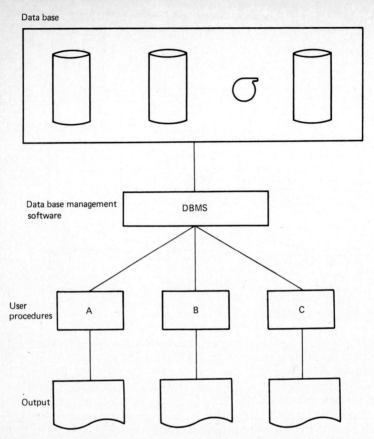

Fig. 10.2 Data processing using a data base management system

or representation when the same item is used in more than one application, and the determination where possible of the frequencies and volumes concerned.

The aim of this analysis phase should be to observe and record the fundamental items of data – people, objects, events – involved in the organisation's activities and how they are related to one another. So far as possible this should be done without dependence on the way data processing is currently carried out.

The resulting description or model is in essence a *conceptual schema* in the terminology of the ANSI/SPARC Study Group's report (ANSI/SPARC, 1978, pp. 173–91). This important report proposed a 3-level view of a data base system (Fig. 10.3). In the centre is the conceptual schema, which is an application independent and storage independent description of a set of information. An *external schema* is a view of the information as seen by one user or group and, as we have already observed, a number of different external schemas may relate to the unique conceptual schema. Finally an *internal schema* is a description of how the data on which the information is based is actually stored.

It has proved difficult to formulate a precise definition of a conceptual schema. To call it 'a description of the real world' is to demand something which is impracticable in its full generality. On the other hand 'a description of the information in a data base system' is too specific, and implies a description of an

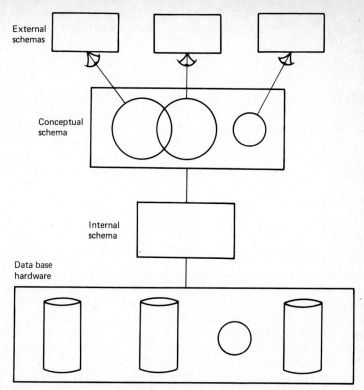

Fig. 10.3 Architecture of the ANSI/SPARC model of a data base system

established data base rather than a model of a system of information which a data base will **subsequently** represent.

A definition which attempts to introduce the dynamic aspect of information systems is that 'a conceptual schema is a formal model of the set of laws which are necessary to specify what information may enter a proposed data base and what transactions may be performed on that information'. More briefly, 'a conceptual schema is a description of a part of the real world and how it evolves'.

At the practical level, the definition of a conceptual schema is complicated by the fact that there are at present no well defined tools for this purpose. Three different types of model have been used in existing data base management systems (the so-called hierarchical, network and relational methods, which we shall describe in more detail later in the chapter) but all these generate system definitions somewhere between the conceptual and internal schema levels. In other words each system imposes some restriction on the data structures and/or data transformations which may be defined.

The consequence of this state-of-the-art in data base technology is that two phases can be identified in the definition of a data base system. The first is a *data analysis* phase, which leads to the construction of some form of conceptual schema or data model for the data resources of the organisation concerned. This model must then be mapped on to a 'logical data base design'. In other words it must be transformed into a new model which satisfies the constraints of the particular DBMS which is to be used for the implementation. An analogy can be drawn with the transformation of a problem definition into a coded program in which rules must be obeyed about, say, the shape of arrays or the specification of procedure parameters.

10.4   A methodology for data analysis

A number of different methodologies have been proposed for data analysis. To illustrate some of the concepts involved, the following sections describe one approach which has proved successful in practice. The principles of the method resemble those of the entity relationship model proposed by Chen (1976, pp. 9–36) and the analysis is carried out in two phases – entity analysis, which identifies the fundamental objects of the system and their relationships, and functional analysis which identifies the transformations which are performed on those objects.

The following two sections are based on a paper by Shave (1981, pp. 42–47) – see also Palmer, (1978).

10.4.1   Entity analysis

The first step is to attempt to identify all the different types of *entity* or basic object which are involved in the system. An entity *type* is a generic term representing a set of items (which may be empty); each item of the set is one *occurrence* of the entity type. Entity types provide a classification of the items in a system, but are not themselves classified. Thus entity types can represent widely different sets of items, such as people, objects, concepts or even events – for example the types Student, Book, Course, Registration.

The occurrences of an entity type will in general be distinguished by the distinctive values of certain properties. Each entity type will possess one or more characteristic *attributes* whose differing values provide one means of identifying the separate occurrences of that type – for example, a student name, a book number, a course code or a registration year.

The next task is to consider whether a *relationship* exists between a pair of identified entity types. The relationship may once again take many different forms, and its identification simply reflects some natural structure in the data. The connection may involve, for example, ownership, propinquity, similarity, structure or sequence. More than one relationship type can exist between two entity types (e.g. the entity types House and Person can be related by Ownership and/or by Occupation). A relationship may also involve only one entity type (e.g. an involuted relationship Sibling between two occurrences of the entity type Person). Each relationship has a *degree*, which may be one-to-one, one-to-many in either direction, or many-to-many. These are described more briefly as $(1, 1)$, $(1, n)$, or (m, n) relationships respectively. A one-to-many relationship between types A and B means that each occurrence of A (the *owner*) may be associated with many occurrences of B (the *member*) but each occurrence of B is related to a unique occurrence of A.

The objective is to record only **direct** relationships. For instance, direct relationships exist between the entities Parent and Child, and between Child and School, but the relationships between Parent and School is indirect – it exists only by virtue of the child.

The objects and concepts of a system do not fall irrevocably into one of the three categories of entity, attribute or relationship type. A classic example is provided by data which refers to marriages. The concept of marriage could be regarded as an entity type (with attributes such as date, place, name of bride and bridegroom), or as an attribute type (a status associated with the entity type Person) or as a relationship type (connecting occurrences of the entity types Man and Woman). One of the tasks of the data analyst is to decide which of these viewpoints is the most appropriate within the system he is considering.

This intrusion of system semantics into the modelling process is perfectly proper; it means only that the model is being developed within its overall context, not that it has become application dependent. Any object may appear in different roles, according to the viewpoint from which it is observed, and the objective of data analysis is to avoid representing the object in the model in a way which is applicable only to one aspect or application of the system. In this respect an entity type provides the most flexible form of definition.

It will be apparent that the definitions which are formulated in the initial stages of the process of entity analysis may in practice be reconsidered as the nature and scope of the data becomes more apparent. For example, Contract may initially be defined as a relationship type between the entities Customer and Company; however, the nature of a contract may determine the department to which the work is allocated and the stock required. This would imply that Contract is more suitably regarded as an entity type in its own right, participating in relationships with Customer, Company, Department and Stock.

Once the definitions have been agreed, they can be illustrated by constructing an entity model of the system. To demonstrate this, consider the following simple scenario.

A city council or local education authority (LEA) appoints a Governing Body for each of its colleges. Each college employs a Principal and the staff are organised into departments. Each course run by a college is the responsibility of a single department but it may be taught by more than one member of staff. Students who apply to a college must have appropriate qualifications and provide a guarantee of financial support from a parent or local authority. On entry, each student is allocated one member of staff as his tutor and registers for one or more courses. For each course which he joins he is allocated a numbered textbook from a stock associated with each course.

From this information the following types may be defined

Entity types	Relationship types and their degree		
LEA	LEA	Governing Body	$1:n$
Governing Body	LEA	Student	$1:n$
College	Governing Body	College	$1:1$
Principal	College	Principal	$1:1$
Staff	College	Department	$1:n$
Department	College	Student	$1:n$
Course	Department	Staff	$1:n$
Student	Department	Course	$1:n$
Qualification	Staff	Course	$m:n$
Parent	Staff	Student	$1:n$
Registration	Course	Registration	$1:n$
Book allocation	Course	Book stock	$1:n$
Book stock	Student	Registration	$1:n$
	Student	Qualification	$1:1$
	Parent	Student	$1:n$
	Registration	Book allocation	$1:1$

Attribute types have been omitted from this example for clarity but, on the basis of the brief description above, it would be reasonable to define Principal, Qualification and Book allocation as attributes of College, Student and Registration respectively, rather than as entity types.

The entity model corresponding to these definitions is shown in Fig. 10.4. An oval box is used to indicate an entity type as a distinction from the rectangular box commonly used to represent a record at the storage level. A delta notation is used for a multivalued relationship in preference to an arrowhead in order to emphasise that access to occurrences of entities may be made in either direction of the relationship. A broken line in the representation of a relationship indicates that occurrences of the adjoining entity type may exist without participating in the relationship. Thus every student must have a member of staff as his tutor, but not every member of staff will act in this capacity. By contrast, a local authority may not be sponsoring any students and a student (e.g. a foreign student) may not be sponsored by any local authority; the arc in the diagram shows, however, that every student must have a sponsored relationship with either a local authority or a parent.

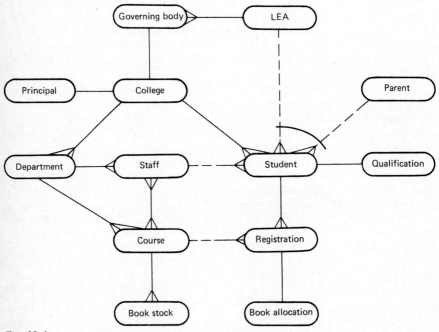

Fig. 10.4

In practice, before a model such as this is constructed, a more detailed knowledge of the system would be obtained by discussion than is represented by the brief description given above. This would help to clarify the semantics of the data; whether, for example, the relationship between a college and members of its staff always occurs via their department, as shown, or whether a further direct relationship should be included in the model.

Attributes, even where they are defined, are commonly omitted from the entity model diagram since they do not add to an appreciation of its structure.

The functional model is shown in Fig. 10.6. Those entity and relationship occurrences which are created by the function are shown with broken lines.

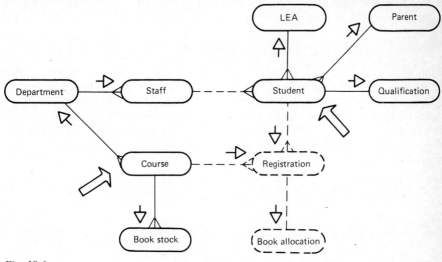

Fig. 10.6

A practical difficulty in functional analysis is to choose a suitable level of interest at which functions are to be defined. At one extreme the entire system is a 'registration function' or a 'payroll function'. At the other extreme, too much detail may lead to an undesirable mimicry of existing processing methods. A guide can be obtained by matching functional models with the entity model; also the level should be such that the objective of a function remains unaltered even if the method of doing it is changed. Thus one might consider a function 'book issue', which requires the identification of a book, a borrower and the date of issue, but the analysis would be likely to ignore details such as the classification of the book or the method of processing the borrower's ticket.

10.5 The conceptual schema and logical data base models

The methodology which has been described in the preceding sections is a highly practical but not unique way of preparing an overall model of an organisation's data resources. Some methodologies, for example, would allow attributes to be associated with relationships as well as with entities. Another model, proposed by Bachman (Bachman and Daya, 1977, pp. 464–76), introduces the concept of a role in addition to the types already present. Thus any occurrence of an entity type (e.g. a person) may be associated with two or more occurrences of a role type (e.g. as parent, employee, youth leader).

In each case the aim is to create a *conceptual schema*, or model, for the organisation. This must now be transformed into a logical data base model.

Since this book is not primarily concerned with data base systems we shall not consider any commercial DBMS in detail. However, we will describe the principles of the three major approaches which have been adopted, showing the limitations which these impose on the conceptual model and indicating how these limitations can be overcome. We will use a unifying example for this purpose, and in a student textbook it is appropriate to base it on a student environment. (A comparable example in a commercial context could refer to Foreman, Employee, Project, Job, etc. in place of Tutor, Student, Degree, Course ...)

10.6 Network data base systems

The most widely adopted system architecture stems from the report of the Database Task Group (CODASYL, 1971), which has led to implementations such as IDMS (available on IBM and ICL computers), DMS1100 (Univac) and IDS (Honeywell). These systems are often called *network* data base systems, a name derived from the data structures which they support, but this use of the word is quite distinct from the communications networks discussed in the previous chapter.

The fundamental concept in CODASYL systems is that of a *set*. A *set type* may be defined as an association between two distinct record types (Fig. 10.7). One of the record types is the *owner* of the set, and the other is a *member*. (There may be more than one member type.) An *occurrence* of a record type is a specific set of values which satisfy the definition of that record type; for example, if the record type student is defined to contain a name and a year-of-study, then Jones, 2 and Smith, 3 are two occurrences of student.

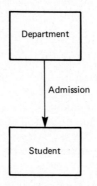

Fig. 10.7 A CODASYL set

An occurrence of a set type consists of precisely one occurrence of its owner together with zero or more occurrences of each member. For example, Fig. 10.8 shows two occurrences of the set ADMISSION as defined by the diagram in Fig. 10.7. Fig. 10.7 is called a data structure or Bachman diagram. Fig. 10.8 is an occurrence diagram. In a structure diagram (Fig. 10.7) the direction of the arrow is significant since it always leads from the owner of the set to the member; however, the arrows in an occurrence diagram have no significance apart from encircling diagramatically one occurrence of a set type. In particular they do not imply anything about the implementation of the set, which may use a forward chain, a 2-way chain, or a pointer array.

The CODASYL rules allow considerable freedom in building structures of sets. In particular, a record type which is a member of one set can be an owner of another set (which allows hierarchies to develop) and a record type may be either an owner or a member in more than one set (which introduces non-

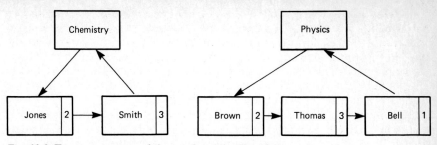

Fig. 10.8 Two occurrences of the set shown in Fig. 10.7

hierarchical networks). These rules are illustrated by the structure diagrams in Fig. 10.9, where STUDENT is a member record of three sets, DEPARTMENT is an owner record of two sets and STAFF is a member of the set EMPLOY-MENT but an owner of the set TUTOR.

By contrast, it is worth re-emphasising two important restrictions on sets, since these form significant constraints on the mapping from a conceptual model. First of all, a set may not have the same record type for both owner and member. This excludes recursive or *involuted sets* such as Fig. 10.10, which represents a managerial structure. Secondly, a member record must have a unique owner in any one set (so that no student in Fig. 10.8 can be admitted by both the chemistry and the physics departments). This also prevents any direct representation of an (*m, n*) relationship between two entities, such as STUDENT and COURSE (a student may attend many courses, and a course contains many students).

To overcome these constraints, CODASYL data base designers make use of *link* records. These records often represent events rather than objects, though

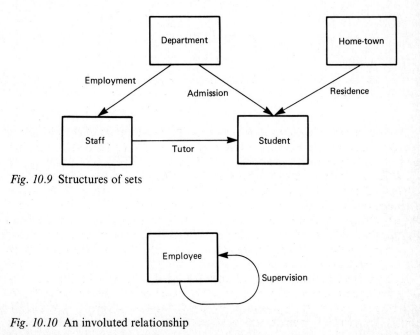

Fig. 10.9 Structures of sets

Fig. 10.10 An involuted relationship

it has to be admitted that the definition of a link record is sometimes somewhat artificial. Two examples are shown in Fig. 10.11*a* and *b*. The (m, n) relationship between STUDENT and COURSE is broken into two $(1, n)$ relationships by introducing the link record ENROLMENT. Any occurrence of this record concerns a particular student and a particular course, but both a student and a course will be associated with several enrolments. ENROLMENT thus participates as a member in two distinct CODASYL sets.

The involuted relationship of supervision is represented by defining a record type SUBORDINATE. Since it is defined as a distinct type it may participate in both the two sets shown, but in practice it will be a dummy record containing little or no data. The IDENTITY set type will be a $(1, 1)$ relationship, and hence any occurrence of EMPLOYEE (on the right) can be associated with a unique occurrence of SUBORDINATE and hence with a unique occurrence of EMPLOYEE (on the left). This enables the supervisor of an employee to be determined. Conversely, given any supervisor, we can access all his SUBORDINATE records through the SUPERVISION set and then obtain details of each one by using the IDENTITY set to retrieve the corresponding EMPLOYEE record.

The overall definition of a CODASYL data base is contained in its *schema*, which is written in the Data Description Language (DDL). Besides set and record descriptions this also specifies items such as the ordering of sets, member-

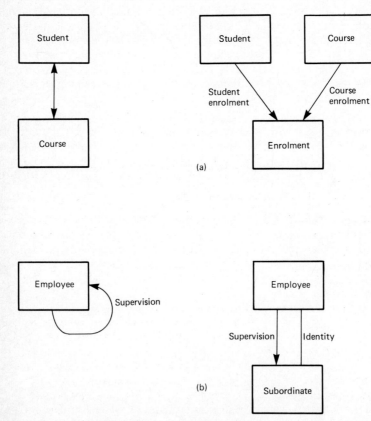

Fig. 10.11 Overcoming constraints on set construction

ship class of records (i.e. rules governing insertion and deletion of occurrences), 'areas' of storage (which enable record types to be grouped physically for efficiency of access) and validation or privacy procedures.

The reader will observe that some of these items bring the CODASYL schema close to the internal schema level as defined in the ANSI/SPARC 3-level data model. Besides this overall description, a view of the data base tailored to the needs of a particular user – an external schema in the ANSI/SPARC terminology – is provided in CODASYL systems by defining a *subschema*. The CODASYL report describes this as 'a consistent and logical subset of the schema from which it is drawn'. Among the changes to a schema that can be made in a subschema are that a user can rename areas, sets, records, or data-items, he may re-order the data-items within a record type and he may alter the access strategy which is used within a set. In addition the declaration of any areas, sets, records or data-items of the schema may be omitted provided the subschema remains self-consistent. This permits a measure of privacy and confidentiality to be imposed if the subschema definition is given **to** the user rather than constructed **by** him.

Finally, operations on the data base by users (which always take place via some subschema) are specified in terms of a Data Manipulation Language (DML). This includes commands such as *FIND, GET, STORE, MODIFY, CONNECT, DISCONNECT* and *USE*. The DML is not a stand-alone system. Instead it serves as an interface between a host programming language (such as Fortran or Cobol) in which a problem is stated and the data base which the user wishes to access.

10.7   Hierarchical data base systems

The following discussion will refer to IBM's Information Management System (IMS) which is much the most common example (though not the only one) of the hierarchical approach to data base design. The reader is warned that the terminology of IMS differs somewhat from the standard practice in other systems, and hence for some of the IMS terms we will indicate alternative names which may be more familiar.

The simplest form of IMS structure is a *physical data base* (tree). Each node of the physical data base is a *segment type* (record type) which may contain a number of named *fields*. A segment type at one level has a *parent-child* relationship with each segment type at its immediate subordinate level. Each child segment type must have a unique parent in the physical data base, and there is a unique root segment type at the highest level. Every physical data base (PDB) thus has a tree format (Fig. 10.12).

A physical data base is defined by a data base description (DBD) which also partly specifies its organisation, but the term physical is misleading and does not imply that the DBD is at storage level. An IMS model will normally contain a number of DBDs.

An occurrence of a physical data base is called a physical data base record (PDBR). An occurrence of a segment type is called a *segment* and there may be zero, one or more segments of a given type in a PDBR. However, a child segment may not exist unless its parent segment is also present. Two segments of the same type and with the same parent are called *physical twins*. There is no restriction

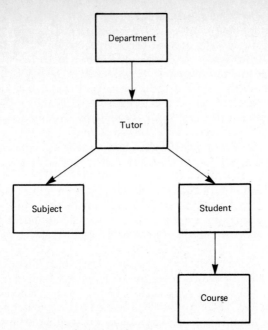

Fig. 10.12 An IMS physical data base (PDB) for academic data

in principle on the number of levels which a physical data base may contain. Fig. 10.13 shows a PDBR which corresponds to the structure in Fig. 10.12.

In the simplest organisation, a PDBR is stored in order of occurrence within levels; that is, in Fig. 10.13, all data relating to the tutor Smith is stored before data relating to the tutor Brown and within this, Smith's subject is stored before data relating to the student Thomas, which in turn precedes data relating to Kent. This is known as the primary processing sequence.

If an IMS model was restricted to a set of disjoint physical data bases there would be serious problems in mapping most conceptual models, since these do not in general fall into disjoint submodels. However, this difficulty is overcome by the important concept of a *logical data base*. This is a hierarchy which is defined in terms of one or more existing physical data bases. It has no existence in its own right, i.e. if physical data bases are deleted any logical data base defined on them will also vanish, nor does it have any segments of its own but extra pointers are added to existing segments to provide the desired structure.

As an example, we might define a physical data base containing administrative details of a college as shown in Fig. 10.14. When discussing halls of residence we wish to refer to students, about whom full details are already recorded in an academic physical data base (Fig. 10.12). Clearly it would be wasteful to duplicate all the student data in the administrative data base. The solution is to define a logical data base which consists of the whole administrative PDB together with an additional 'logical parent-logical child' relationship which is indicated in Fig. 10.14 by a dotted line. This enables all data in the STUDENT segment and any of its dependent segments to be accessed as though they were part of the administrative PDB.

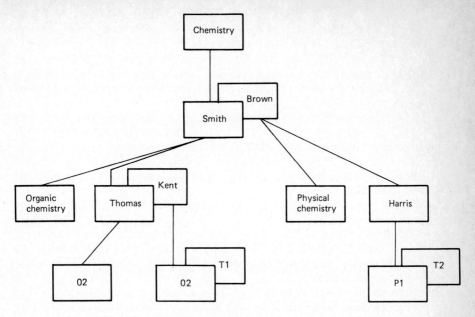

Fig. 10.13 A physical data base record (PDBR) corresponding to Fig. 10.12

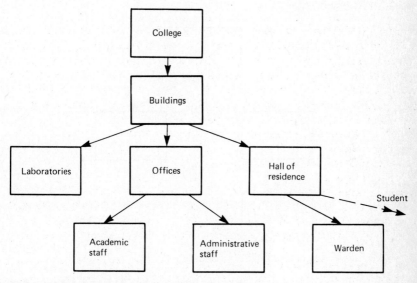

Fig. 10.14 A PDB for administrative data

It is worth noting that the dotted line can represent a bidirectional relationship if a second logical data base is defined which consists of the academic PDB together with STUDENT as a logical parent of HALL OF RESIDENCE. This would enable a department to retrieve data about the Hall and Warden where any given student is accommodated – for example, to send official examination notices.

The purpose of a logical data base can be summarised by saying that it provides a user with an alternative view of the data. This may suggest that logical data bases correspond to ANSI/SPARC's external schema, and to some extent this is true, but in practice they usually play an essential part in forming an IMS model of the conceptual schema itself. The nearest equivalent of an external schema is the *program specification block* which specifies which are the data bases and segment types that a program may access.

To allow further flexibility in the basis on which a data base is accessed, IMS provides a *secondary index* facility. This is essentially an extension of the concept which we have considered previously in the simpler case of an inverted file. The IMS user may index a segment not only on the basis of any field of that segment but the index can also be on the basis of any field in a dependent segment of the physical data base.

Thus in Fig. 10.12, if FACULTY is a field of DEPARTMENT (but not the sequence or prime key field) and HOME TOWN is a similar field of STUDENT, then secondary indexes for the Academic PDB may be defined on FACULTY or HOME TOWN or both. The effect of an index on FACULTY is simply to provide a secondary processing sequence based on this field in addition to the primary sequence defined initially.

An index on HOME TOWN would have a more far-reaching effect, giving the user a new view of the hierarchy with STUDENT as the root. The structure which would be seen by the user in this case is shown in Fig. 10.15. Notice that both dependents and antecedents of STUDENT can be accessed, but the latter appear in reversed order.

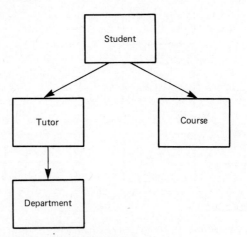

Fig. 10.15 A new view gained from a secondary index

Although secondary indexes may appear to be (and are) of value for particular problems, this mode of access can be used only if suitable indexes have been included as part of the overall data base description (DBD). Ideally this feature should be part of the storage-level schema and the result is to impair the efficiency of operations which do not require the secondary indexes.

For the primary processing sequence IMS provides a number of alternative storage organisations which offer the user a choice between direct and sequential storage, with or without an index. Although all these facilities are powerful, the

IMS user does not have quite as much flexibility to choose or 'navigate' his own path through the data base structure as is available to the user of a CODASYL system. Opinions differ on the extent to which a user should be able to be, or allowed to be, aware of the physical organisation of a data base.

10.8 Relational data base models

Relational systems provide the highest level, most storage independent approach to data base management which is currently available. The essential feature is that all data is seen by the user as residing in tables or *relations*. The overall body of data is broken down into small logical subareas (by the process of normalisation described below) so that each table contains data for a single subarea. Examples of some typical relations are shown in Table 10.1(a) the *key* in italics and a typical content for one of these is illustrated in Table 10.1(b).

The heading of each column is called an *attribute* of the relation and the values within that column must all belong to a common type or *domain*. Two or more distinct attributes may draw their values from the same domain (e.g. Head and Faculty are both based on a string domain). The number of attributes is the *degree* of the relation. Each row of the relation is called a *tuple* and the number of tuples is the *cardinality* of the relation.

A formal definition is

given a collection of domains $D_1, D_2, \ldots, D_n$ (not necessarily distinct), a relation R on these n domains is a set of ordered n-tuples $(d_1, d_2, \ldots, d_n)$ such that $d_i \, \varepsilon \, D_i, i = 1, 2, \ldots, n$.

An attribute whose values uniquely identify the tuples of a relation is called the key of the relation. In some cases the key is formed from a group of attributes.

Whereas the network and hierarchical systems go to great lengths to represent all types of connections within a set of information, the relational systems use just one method. Each relation represents an association between certain items of data; for example, there is an association between Faculty, Department names and certain people who are Heads. Outside a relation, the only method of establishing an association is when two tuples (rows) have related

Table 10.1 (a) Five typical relations

DEPT (*Dept-name,* Head, Faculty)
TUTOR (*Dept-name, Tutor-name,* Salary, Date-of-appointment)
STUDENT (*Dept-name, Tutor-name, Student-name,* Home-town, Entry-year, Degree-title)
OPTIONS (*Degree-title, Course-code,* Dept. name)
COURSE (*Course-code,* Course-name, Start-date, Length, Frequency)

(b) some tuples of the DEPT relation

DEPT:			
	Anatomy	Stubbs	Medicine
	Botany	Jones	Science
	Economics	Keynes	Social Science
	History	Taylor	Arts
	Philosophy	Kant	Arts
	Physics	Rutherford	Science

---

values for some common attributes. Thus we can deduce that certain students will belong to a particular Faculty when equal Department names occur in the DEPT and STUDENT relations.

This recognition of an association is the method used to create any new relations required to answer user enquiries. In other words, we can say that a relation is the only structure allowed by the system. All data, whether it is input data, intermediate data (i.e. in working storage) or a result, is held in this form. The data base management system will maintain consistency among its permanent relations, but not between them and transient relations unless the latter are redefined on a permanent basis.

The operations which may be performed on relations are

SELECT   Choose all tuples in a relation for which some predicate is satisfied, e.g.

 SELECT DEPT *WHERE* Faculty = "Arts"

 or

 SELECT TUTOR *WHERE* Salary < $10 000

PROJECT   a new relation is formed which contains only the specified attributes of an existing relation. Any duplicate tuples which occur as a result of this contraction of the relation are deleted e.g.

 PROJECT COURSE *OVER* Course-code, Start-date

JOIN   Given two relations which have a common attribute a join is a new relation containing all tuples which can be concatenated from the equal values in the common domain. Thus if $A(P,Q,R)$ and $B(R,S,T)$ are two relations, the join of A and B on R is a relation $C(P, Q, R, S, T)$ which contains tuples of the form (p, q, r_a, s, t) where $(p, q, r_a) \varepsilon A$, $(r_b, s, t) \varepsilon B$, and $r_a = r_b$.

In addition there is a *DIVIDE* operator, which we will not discuss here, and it is possible to apply the standard set operations of Union, Difference and Intersection.

Some examples of the use of these relational operators are given in Table 10.2. Examples such as these which use the relational operators explicitly are said to be using *relational algebra*. The reader will notice that this is a procedural approach in which the user expresses **how** the required relational result is to be constructed.

Relational calculus is a higher-level user interface in which the user merely states a **definition** of the required relation in the form of a predicate. Most relational implementations use this form of language, and the examples in Table 10.3 (for the same problems as before) are based on IBM's SQL language for System R.

Table 10.2 Inquiries using relational algebra

---

1   Obtain the names of all students in the Dept of Computing who live in Birmingham.

        S1 : = *PROJECT* STUDENT *OVER* Dept-name, Student-name, Home-town

RESULT: = *SELECT* S1 *WHERE* Dept-name = "Computing"
                                     AND Home-town = "Birmingham"

2   Find the head(s) of department for the student(s) named Jones.

        S1 : = *SELECT* STUDENT *WHERE* Student-name = "Jones".

        S2 : = *PROJECT* S1 *OVER* Dept-name, Student-name

        S3 : = *PROJECT* DEPT *OVER* Dept-name, Head

        S4 : = *JOIN* S2, S3 *OVER* Dept-name

RESULT: = *PROJECT* S4 *OVER* Head, Student-name

3   Find the name and department of all students taking course C2.

        S1 : = *PROJECT* STUDENT *OVER* Student-name, Dept-name, Degree-title

        S2 : = *SELECT* OPTIONS *WHERE* Course-code = "C2"

        S3 : = *PROJECT* S2 *OVER* Degree-title

        S4 : = *JOIN* S1 *AND* S3 *OVER* Degree-title

RESULT: = *PROJECT* S4 *OVER* Student-name, Dept-name

Table 10.3 Inquiries using relational calculus

---

1   *SELECT* Student-name
        FROM   STUDENT
        WHERE Dept-name = "Computing" *AND* Home-town = "Birmingham"

2   *SELECT* Head
        FROM   DEPT
        WHERE Dept-name =
                 SELECT Dept-name
                 FROM STUDENT
                 WHERE Student-name = "Jones"

3   *SELECT* Dept-name, Student-name
        FROM   STUDENT
        WHERE Degree-title =
                 SELECT Degree-title
                 FROM OPTIONS
                 WHERE Course-code = "C2"

10.8.1 Normalisation

So far we have taken all the relations as given, but how does one choose the most appropriate attributes for each relation? The short answer is that we wish to minimise redundancy, to reduce the need for restructuring relations if new types of data arise and to disengage logically distinct aspects of the data so that modifications which concern only one area can be made without causing side effects. To achieve these objectives Codd (Codd, 1970, pp. 377–87) defined a step-by-step process of *normalisation* in which a given set of relations is refined into new sets which have a progressively simpler and more regular structure. Before considering the details we will demonstrate some of the undesirable situations which the process is designed to avoid.

Suppose that tutor names are unique within a department, that student names are unique within a tutor group and that we begin with a large relation COLLEGE containing the following data

Dept. name, Head, Faculty, Tutor name, Salary,
Student name, Home-Town, LEA (Local Education Authority), Registration date.

The registration date of a student is determined only by the initial letter of his name and is independent of his department and tutor.Then some typical problems are

(i)   data about departments and tutors has to be repeated for every student,

(ii)   the LEA of a student is determined by his home town, but if no student is currently living in, say, Bath, there is no means of recording the fact that Avon County Council is the LEA for this town,

(iii)   it is impossible to enter a student into the data base without knowing and recording the name of his head of department and the salary of his tutor,

(iv)   if registration dates are changed, then every tuple in the relation must be modified.

These difficulties occur because the relation COLLEGE includes data from a number of logically distinct or orthogonal areas. COLLEGE is described as an unnormalised relation and the problems are overcome by a series of normalisation steps.

First normal form (1NF) is obtained by creating separate relations for any repeating groups. In COLLEGE, tutor data is repeated for every student and department data is repeated for every tutor. We therefore define

STUDENT 1
(*Dept-name, Tutor-name, Student-name*, Home-Town, LEA, Registration-date)
TUTOR
(*Dept-name, Tutor-name,* Salary)
DEPT.
(*Dept-name,* Head, Faculty)

These three relations are all in 1NF. Their keys are italicised.

Second normal form (2NF) is obtained by creating a separate relation for any attributes which depend on only a subset of the key of their relation.

Registration-date is a case in point. We define

STUDENT 2
(*Dept-name, Tutor-name, Student-name,* Home-Town, LEA)

REGISTRATION
(*Student-initial*, Registration-date)

Third normal form (3NF) is obtained by creating a separate relation for any attributes which depend on some other non-key attribute(s) within their relation (i.e. which are only transitively dependent on the prime key).

The LEA attribute, which is determined by Home-Town, is an example of this. We define

STUDENT 3
(*Dept-name, Tutor-name, Student-name,* Home-Town)
AUTHORITY
(*Home-Town,* LEA)

Finally, therefore, we have the relations

TUTOR, DEPT, REGISTRATION, STUDENT3, AUTHORITY

all of which are in third normal form, and the anomalies (i) – (iv) have all been overcome.

Although this set of data has now been expressed in a satisfactory way, difficulties may still occur even when all relations are in 3NF – typically, if a key value uniquely determines a set of data rather than an individual item (for example, a tutor's children or his publications). A *fourth normal form* has been defined for this purpose by Fagin (Fagin, 1977, pp. 262–78) and readers are referred to the relevant literature for details.

The important point is that the normalisation process is concerned with the meaning of the data which is to be recorded and research is still continuing on the best way to capture this within the relational model. The relational approach has important advantages in simplicity of concept, storage-independence and a sound theoretical basis, but the use of a single type of structure can be difficult for the user and leads to complex consistency constraints. It is interesting that recent work by Borkin (Borkin, 1980, pp. 47–64) has advocated a *semantic relation data model* in which tabular structures are associated with a semantic graph. The aim is to capture the understanding of an application which a graphical model provides (as used in the network approach discussed earlier) while maintaining the high-level description of operations on the data which is given by relational systems.

10.9   Data administration

We have devoted most of this chapter to a discussion of the concepts and techniques of data bases, in order to give students a good overall understanding of the methods available for this important application of computing. However, since a data base provides a service to a user community there are also important managerial and administrative aspects involved.

We remarked at the beginning of the chapter that the essence of using a data base approach was to regard data as a resource of a company or organisation as a whole and not the private preserve of a particular department. Since no one subgroup can claim authority for data, except as delegated by higher authority, the corollary of the decision to treat data as a central resource is that responsibility for it must be vested in some central (and high-level) appointment. This is the role of a *data administrator*. This job is a new one, and still relatively rare in all but the largest organisations. The duties of the post are not as yet generally agreed, but some or all of the following will normally be included

- cost-benefit studies of data handling methods (including data base systems) in the context of the parent organisation

- data analysis

- design and maintenance of the corporate data model

- establishment and maintenance of coding systems, data standards and documentation

- data dictionary facilities (see below)

- rules for data ownership

- resolution of conflicts of interest and decisions on trade-off strategies

- data security and access controls

It should be noted that the data administrator is **not** responsible for the details of data **base** management. These are the concern of a separate second-level post. the *data base administrator,* whose responsibilities will include

- design of the logical model (as distinct from the corporate data model)

- integration of new applications

- data base consistency and validity

- recovery procedures

- performance monitoring

- data base reorganisation for optimal efficiency

- data base documentation and procedures

Although both these posts are important, the data administrator has the more far-reaching and delicate role to play; it is a pity that companies who have made such an appointment have not always given it the status it deserves. The adoption of a data base approach in place of a long-established application-oriented system inevitably leads to many changes in methods of work and standard conventions. These changes mean inconvenience and extra effort for staff, whose resistance is frequently based as much on legitimate practical objections as on any irrational prejudices.

We have already remarked, in Chapter 1, on the importance of personal factors in the development of successful computing systems and the data base area is no exception. The data administrator will require both the authority to take decisions and great tact to win support for them, particularly when users' interests are to some extent initially incompatible.

Many of the decisions which are needed in adopting and implementing a data base system have important consequences which extend well beyond the mere data processing activities of an organisation. Not the least important of these is the cost of hardware, software, staff retraining, workshop or stores reorganisation, etc. Hence the data administrator must not only have the authority to control departmental use of data, but also the status and character to guide (though not to direct) senior management. In some cases this will involve meetings at board level.

It is little wonder if it is said that the only people who can fill the post of data administrator successfully are already managing directors!

10.10 Data dictionaries

In taking a high-level view of the data resources of an organisation, the data administrator is primarily concerned with the **meaning** of the data, rather than the details of its implementation (which are the concern of a data base administrator). For this purpose he will need to establish and maintain a precise definition of each entity, attribute and relationship in the data model (or whatever are the equivalent terms in the methodology he uses for data analysis). Synonyms and homonyms which have become established by usage must also be recorded – for example an 'account' to a marketing department often means the same thing as a 'customer' does to the finance office, while 'product-code' may refer to a supplier's number, a sales number or a shelf number. Another important consideration will be the specification of inter- and intra-data consistency constraints, e.g. that an order cannot exist unless it is related to some customer or that 'quantity in stock' is necessarily non-negative.

In this way the process of data analysis generates a considerable body of information of its own – data about the data, or meta-data to use the technical phrase – which must itself be organised, updated and made available when required. This is the purpose of a data dictionary system. In its most sophisticated form it has been aptly if idealistically described as 'a data base for a data base'. At the other extreme it could be no more than a well arranged manual filing system. In practice there are a number of commercially available data dictionary systems which provide automated data supervision to a greater or lesser degree.

The facilities available in data dictionaries vary considerably, but the documentation which can be obtained could include

- lists of cross-references of entity, attribute and relationship types, together with their properties

- lists and definitions of functions and events including frequency information

- for each entity type, a list of all functions which use it

- for each function, a list of all access paths and entity types which it requires

- keyword indexes

- synonyms and homonyms

- directories specific to particular departments

Although the data dictionary may be established in the first instance to assist a data administrator during the preliminary data analysis phase, it will be apparent that the dictionary can and should be extended to support data base implementation in its widest sense. It then becomes a tool for the data base administrator as well and, indeed, for users generally. Its objectives can thus be defined as the documentation of an organisation's data and of the implementation of that data, in order to form a basis for standardisation, co-ordination and communication between data base designers, programmers and users.

As an example of the contents of a data dictionary, some typical items for each entity type would be

- name, definition, description, and synonyms

- associated attributes and relationships

- ownership

- other application areas (departments)

- key or means of identification

- privacy and deletion rights

- statistics – volume, frequency of creation, deletion or modification, etc.

- timespan, currency status, historical versions

- format for output

Similar data would be recorded for each type of attribute, relationship, function and transaction.

10.11 Data protection

One of the worries most frequently expressed when the use of data bases is discussed is whether the integrity and security of the data can be maintained. Integrity means that the data is accurate, consistent and free from accidental corruption. Security means the prevention of unauthorised retrieval, modification or destruction.

10.11.1 Security

We shall not enter the ethical and political discussion about an individual's 'right to know', but concern over the accuracy and confidentiality of sensitive financial, medical or criminal records is entirely understandable and proper. In the commercial and scientific fields too these matters are equally important. While it cannot be said, unfortunately, that fears are groundless, very considerable efforts are devoted in data base software to maintaining the highest possible level of data protection.

Data security is essentially a matter of maintaining checks against unauthorised access at a sufficient number of points to be effective whilst allowing authorised users sufficient freedom. Some possible points of control are

- terminal access (unlocked by a badge or key)

- operating system identification (password)

- subschema contents or user view

- specific relations, entity types, or access paths

- specific functions or programs

Just as for conventional files, users may be classified into categories and different types of access allowed for each category. Typical categories are

- the data base administrator

- the 'owner' of the data

- individual users identified by name

- groups of users identified by affiliation (e.g. student registered for course "C2")

- all other users

However, the size and complexity of a data base presents problems which are not encountered in smaller-scale conventional systems. For example, security must apply at both logical and physical levels. A local authority data base could contain tenancy records (for the housing department) and family records (for the education department). Access to either could be quite legitimate, but access to both could, by virtue of a common Name attribute, allow information about ethnic backgrounds to be associated with information about housing. A sub-schema definition which does not allow certain combinations of attributes in the same user view may be the solution in this case, but such problems are not easy to solve.

Some other examples of the fine control which may be demanded of a security system are

- a user may be allowed to see just one instance of a record type, and to amend only some of its fields

- a user may amend entries in a student's results record if and only if he is identified as a tutor with the same department code as the student

- only specified users may execute a salary increment function and such users may see only the name and salary fields of the records concerned

- the salary fields of employee records may be accessed only during prime shift time, and then only by finance department staff

The fact that security facilities such as this are demanded does not mean that all of them are or can be provided. There will certainly be a significant cost in the performance efficiency of the system. Nevertheless there is no doubt that flexible and powerful security controls must become an important feature of future DBMS.

10.11.2 Integrity

Constraints on the accuracy and consistency of a data base arise in three ways. Firstly, there are constraints which must be maintained because of the inherent semantics of the data, such as that salaries for employees in Grade X must be between $14 000 and $20 000, or that quantity sold $\leq$ quantity in stock. Secondly, there are constraints imposed on the operation of the data base, to guard against a conflict of transactions. Thirdly, there are procedures to alleviate failure in some parts of the system.

The first type, which we can call *consistency* constraints, can all be specified in the data dictionary. Some of them, but not all, can then be incorporated in the data base schema definition and/or external schema definitions. In present systems, consistency constraints which are checked automatically in this way are usually quite simple. Various methods of implementation are used; in some systems a suitable predicate is attached to each modification command given by the user before it is executed, in others a verification procedure is involved.

It is usually possible for a user to define a new consistency constraint at any time for his own 'view' of the data base. When this happens the DBMS must verify that all existing data satisfies the new criterion and reject the constraint if it does not.

Some constraints may be too complex or too specific to be incorporated in a schema definition and these must be checked by users when writing their programs to interface with the data base.

Transaction constraints are necessary to control simultaneous access (or attempted access) to items in a data base. If one process is performing an operation on a set of data (e.g. calculating interest on customers' accounts or searching for a specified name) then that set of data must not be changed while the operation is in progress (otherwise an item could be extracted at the start of the operation, 'hidden' for a brief period and restored at the end of the operation – hence no interest charged, or a debtor absent!)

For some types of operation there is no objection to another process *reading* the data at the same time provided the data is not modified. In other cases, the first process is itself modifying the data and therefore all other access must be prohibited until the operation is complete.

This type of control is provided by *locks* on sections of the data base. The lock may be shared (other access allowed, but not modification) or exclusive. The problem is to decide on the size of a section. Is it a field, a record (tuple) or a record type (relation)? The larger the section which is locked, the greater the number of processes which will be affected, and the slower the response of the data base. On the other hand if all sections are very small, a large number of locks will have to be managed by the system. Simulation experiments (Ries and Stonebraker, 1977, pp. 233–46) suggest that the locking granularity can be quite coarse, with the total number of locks in the data base kept in the range 10–200.

The duration of the lock is the period during which the data base is, or could be, in an inconsistent state. For instance, if one constituent in a check total is altered, the lock must be maintained until the total itself has been amended. A unit of work which transforms a data base from one consistent state to another is called a *transaction*.

Since locks are set and freed dynamically, provision must be made for deadlock situations in which two transactions each wish to impose a lock on certain data which is already locked by the other. The only possible solution is to undo the work of one transaction so that the other can proceed. Notice that this requires the existence of a transformation log to show what changes must be reversed.

Recovery procedures are designed to cater for either localised failure (for example, of a communication line) or a major collapse which affects significant areas of auxiliary memory. In either case, recovery makes use of checkpoints at which the current processes and the state of their data have been recorded. The system also has available *images* of data values before and/or after each transaction which have been recorded in the transaction logs. By this means it is possible to back-out the recent transactions and revert to a checkpoint at which the data base is known to have been consistent. Periodically a more extensive dump of the data base may be taken as an additional insurance, but this is a time-consuming and disruptive process.

10.12 Distributed data bases

The data base concept evolved during the 1970's in response to the growing volume and complexity of the data processed by many organisations and the need to rationalise this by establishing an integrated view of its logical structure. Yet whatever the need for corporate control over strategic decisions, the centralisation hitherto associated with data bases is often found to be in conflict with a desire to devolve routine responsibilities to local groups. This desire has been fostered by technological developments which have made local computing systems more economically justifiable, such as powerful but cheaper minicomputers, networking facilities and microprocessors.

Furthermore if most of the data has strongly localised relevance, there can be a considerable saving on transmission costs if the processing of the data can also be localised.

There has been considerable progress in distributed processing when applied to a purely local view of data. A distributed data base implies a significantly higher level of sophistication in which a number of autonomous data base systems at different sites are made to co-operate with each other under some form of overall control.

The overall control, to which we may refer logically as a global schema, must contain a logical description of the data which is incorporated in the distributed system (some data may have local status only), the physical site where it is stored and the constraints which must be maintained. Each local site will have its own conceptual or logical schema with which the global schema must be interfaced.

Logically there is a distinct global machine but the physical system may well be at one of the local sites and possibly even run as a distinct process on one of the existing computers.

The constituent data base systems may be homogeneous (e.g. all IMS systems) or heterogeneous. Clearly the former greatly simplifies the task of implementing an overall distributed system, but the latter situation is likely to be much more common in practice. Consider, for example, a large corporation with a number of subsidiary companies, each of which has hitherto organised its own data processing requirements.

Distributed data bases present all the problems of unified systems together with others of their own; for example

- consistency is complicated by the delay and unreliability of communication lines

- what action should be taken if one site is unavailable but the system as a whole remains viable?

- what should be done if the central control is unavailable but a local site is viable?

- should there be a single copy of the global schema or should it too be distributed?

- where should processing take place when data for a request is stored at a number of sites?

- how should data be allocated between sites, by origin, by usage, dynamically? etc.

There are few clear solutions to these problems as yet, though much research is being done. One or two distributed data base systems have been implemented, almost all with homogeneous local sites. It is virtually certain that these will be followed by heterogeneous systems and systems with distributed control, but the form which these will take and the efficiency they will offer remains uncertain.

Questions

Questions 10.1 and 10.4 use notation from the COBOL programming language, in which each new 'level number' indicates a subfield within a field of a record. The phrase 'OCCURS...' indicates repetition of a field. Thus the following diagram and data description correspond to a record A which contains subfields B and E, and where B has further subfields C (repeated) and D.

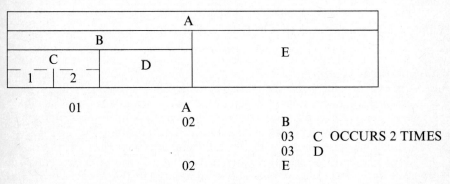

```
01                    A
          02                B
                       03    C  OCCURS 2 TIMES
                       03    D
          02                E
```

10.1 (a) Summarise the major differences between a relation and a traditional file.

(b) Define 'Third Normal Form'.
Convert the record shown below into Third Normal Form, explaining briefly the reason for each step in the conversion and indicating all domains that you select as keys.

```
01   STUDENT-MARKS
  03 STUDENT-NAME
  03 STUDENT-NUMBER
  03 COURSE-ID
  03 COURSE-TITLE
  03 FINAL-YEAR-SUBJECTS        OCCURS 2 TIMES.
     05 COMPULSORY-SUBJECT-ID
     05 COMPULSORY-MARK
     05 OPTION-SUBJECT-ID
     05 OPTION-MARK
  03 PROJECT-TITLE
  03 PROJECT-MARK
```

(c)   Discuss critically the features of Relational Algebra and Relation Calculus for specifying queries to a relational data base management system.   [Thames, 1979]

10.2 (a)   In the context of data bases, define the terms

set
child segment
relation

including the type of data base system to which each applies. In each case state one restriction which must be observed.

(b)   In a relational data base system what do you understand by the process of *normalisation*? State, with an example, any one of the steps involved in converting an unnormalised relation to third normal form.

(c)   Distinguish between the concepts of entity, attribute and relationship in the analysis of data.

Identify the entities and direct relationships in the following environment, and the degree of each relationship. Hence draw a simple entity model to illustrate your analysis, explaining any conventions which you use.

'A building society offers its investors a number of different types of account. An investor may have several accounts provided each is of a different type. The society has a number of branches and each investor is attached to one branch at which details of his account are held. However he is also issued with a passbook for each account and can make a withdrawal at any branch provided he presents his passbook as identification.'   [Bristol, 1981]

10.3 (a)   In CODASYL data base systems

(i)   What is meant by set type and set occurrence?

(ii)   How are many-to-many relationships between records handled?

(b)   A manufacturing organisation has several plants in different parts of the country. Each plant tends to specialise, so that any one project undertaken will be the responsibility of one plant, though several plants may manufacture the same parts. Both customer and internal production orders are controlled as projects.

New products to be undertaken at a factory are batched into a shop order. A part order is raised for each type of component, whenever they are needed, during the production of each project. A part order may cover the requirements of several projects. The part orders, and the operations necessary to produce the parts, are scheduled. This involves the allocation of the operations to work centres, all of which are capable of a range of types of operation, within the factories.

    (i)   List the entities mentioned in the description, noting any synonyms

    (ii)   What relationships exist between these entities, and of what degree are they? Draw a diagram illustrating the relationships

    (iii)   How could the diagram be modified so that it could be mapped directly on to a CODASYL description?

[Thames, 1979]

10.4 (a)   In the context of data bases, what is meant by the terms

    (i)   a relation

    (ii)   functional dependence

    (iii)   relational calculus

(b)   Describe how unnormalised relations can be put into the third normal form. Demonstrate this process on the following COBOL record

```
01  DRUG-MANUFACTURE-AND-DISTRIBUTION
    02  MANUFACTURER-NAME
    02  HEAD-OFFICE-ADDRESS
    02  DRUG-STANDARD-NAME
    02  DISTRIBUTION              OCCURS 30 TIMES.
        03  COUNTRY
        03  BRAND-NAME
        03  PRICE
        03  PATENT-NUMBER
```

Assume that each manufacturer produces a range of drugs, and that each drug has a unique standard name. The drugs are sold in 30 different countries, and in each country a manufacturer has a single brand name, price and patent number for each drug.

(c)   For the relations

AUTHOR (Author's name, Author's address, Age)
PUBLISHER (Publisher's name, Publisher's address)
BOOK (Title, Author's name, Publisher's name)

specify relational algebra expressions to represent the following queries

    (i)   What are the names of all the authors?

    (ii)   For all books, what are the Title, Author's address and Publisher's address?

    (iii)   Which publishers have published books by both MILL and MARX?

[Thames, 1979]

10.5 Explain briefly the principle of the third normal form (3NF) of a collection of data elements. What advantages does 3NF offer the systems analyst when analysing business data with a view to its incorporation into a computerised system?

A company keeps a record of quotations (i.e. prices offered) made by its suppliers for the parts it requires for manufacturing purposes. These are written as lines of a ledger having the following nine column headings: Date, Part Number, Part Description, Supplier Number, Supplier Name, Quotation Price, Supplier Address, Supplier Region code, Region priority rating. Represent these as four relations in 3NF and underline the key elements in each relation. Give the relations. [City, 1980]

10.6 (i) Describe what is meant by a relation and how it differs from a traditional file.

(ii) A relation TIMETABLE is defined on the following domains.

D   Day of the week (1–5)
P   Period within day (1–8)
C   Classroom number
T   Teacher name
S   Student name
L   Lesson identifier (unique)

A tuple (D,P,C,T,S,L) is an element of this relation if at time (D,P) a student S is taught lesson L by teacher T in classroom C. Reduce TIMETABLE to an equivalent set of 3NF relations.

(iii) For the relations

S   (Supplier number, Status, City)
SP   (Supplier number, Part number, Quantity)
P   (Part number, Colour, Weight)

specify the relational algebra expressions to represent the following queries

(a) Get supplier numbers for suppliers who supply part P2
(b) Get supplier numbers for suppliers who supply at least one red part
(c) For each part, get part number and names of all cities where the part may be obtained [Thames, 1980]

10.7 Compare and contrast the problems of security, integrity, and control in batch and real-time systems.

What effect does the use of a data base have on the solution to any of these problems? [Thames, 1980]

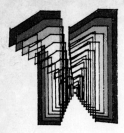

Controls and auditing

In this chapter we are concerned with controls which can be placed on computer based business systems with particular reference to the needs of the auditor. Auditing is a very real constraint for system designers and computer administrators. New legal requirements and growing demands for corporate accountability have forced them to re-examine and improve computer based controls, and there is no doubt that auditing and internal control considerations will be an increasingly major influence on the design of future systems. We shall see that the viewpoints of the auditor and the computer administrator may differ, but that the means by which they achieve their objectives have much in common.

Auditing has two facets: the external audit, which is a legal requirement that firms must undertake every year; and an internal audit function which, by monitoring the operation of a business, can help to control deliberate as well as accidental errors and may also attempt to improve efficiency.

The principal objective of the external audit is to enable independent people, usually a firm of accountants, to ascertain whether, in their opinion, the financial statements on which they are working show a 'true and fair view' of the state of affairs. Hence the steps in the audit process concentrate on identifying those items and activities which affect the overall truth and fairness of the financial reports. Some errors, some questionable activities and some parts of the data processing, may have less attention paid to them on the grounds that they are not material to the overall truth and fairness of the financial statements.

Internal auditing is under the direction and control of management, and in some companies the principal aim will be to prevent fraud (i.e. deliberate errors for personal gain). The internal auditor can keep a constant watch on the organisation and may be able to recommend speedy action to management, once a problem has been detected, whereas the external auditor can only report on fraud once it has happened. To some extent all auditing is preventive – it improves the security and control of systems and may deter individuals from carrying out fraud.

Before discussing the functions of an auditor and the audit approach, it is convenient to recall how a manual accounting system establishes control.

11.1 Internal control in manual accounting systems

In Chapter 4 we saw that manual accounting systems have a number of built-in features to detect errors, such as double-entry book-keeping, control accounts and the subsidiary ledger, the audit trail and communications with customers and suppliers.

A further check which is usually undertaken is the reconciliation of bank statements with the cash balance in the general ledger. Any differences between the two figures should be capable of being explained by differences of timing in the recording of cash transactions. The process is not as simple as it sounds since, as well as cheques entered through the firm's own books but not yet processed by the bank's data processing system, there are bank service charges and customer cheques which have not been cleared because of insufficient funds or because there is a mistake in the cheque itself.

A number of techniques and procedures are used to avoid other errors that cannot be trapped within a manual accounting system. A fundamental principle is that there should be a clear delegation and separation of duties. In part this is due to efficiency considerations (the organisation chart should define these duties and responsibilities), but in part it is a technique designed to make fraud more difficult. The custody of assets, and the record keeping of these assets, must always be clearly segregated if internal control is to be maintained, otherwise the person responsible for inventory could manipulate the physical stocks and also adjust the records. If two separate people are involved, fraud can only be undertaken by collusion of at least two people. Thus, by segregating duties, fraud is made more difficult. Similarly the authorisation of transactions must be separated from the recording of those transactions in the journals, and both should be segregated from posting transactions to the ledgers.

Although these precautions certainly help to reduce errors problems can still arise, so that the person processing a transaction at any particular stage may unwittingly be processing a fraudulent transaction. A pay slip with the amount of overtime over-stated but duly authorised is an error that arises outside the system's ability to detect errors. Other errors are more complex, such as payment against a fictitious invoice from a fictitious supplier. Similarly, although the absence of a receipt for goods is easily checked, the sale of assets at inflated prices is more difficult to detect once the purchase order has been duly authorised. Follow-up of this type of fraud is usually performed by the internal auditors. This illustrates an important type of segregation which is necessary for handling inventories, namely the separation of the purchasing function from the receiving function.

In general the maintenance of internal control requires that proper procedures are followed for the processing of transactions, beginning with proper authorisation. In turn this requires that there should be suitable documentation (prenumbered if necessary), proper accounting records backed by a chart of accounts and a procedures manual. Similarly, there should be adequate physical control over assets and accounting records.

11.2 External auditing

Auditing can be divided into a number of steps. The first step is to understand and record the procedures and controls which comprise an accounting system. Since most data processing areas impinge on the accounting system, this means the auditor will normally have to study most (if not all) of the data processing application areas and the data processing department.

The next stage of the audit process is the evaluation of internal control. The auditor is concerned with a company's internal control (and internal audit function) because if he can place some reliance on internal controls, this may limit the amount of subsequent work. Often an auditor will report on weaknesses he has found in order to help management in carrying out its obligation to establish and maintain controls that ensure the reliability and accuracy of the company's accounting records.

In the job of evaluating internal controls, the auditor makes a distinction between the actual controls (sometimes called *basic controls*) and the administration of those controls (sometimes called *disciplines* over basic controls). The function of basic controls is to ensure that valid transactions are recorded. Disciplines over basic controls (or more simply disciplines) are those features designed to ensure that the basic controls continue to operate properly and they include a number of standard audit principles such as segregation of duties, supervision of the results of one person's work by another, separation of the custody of assets from the accounting responsibility for them and physical arrangements that prevent unauthorised access to assets or accounting records.

Once the internal controls of a system have been evaluated, the auditor will undertake further tests. These are often called *compliance* and *substantive* tests. Compliance tests (sometimes known as functional tests) are tests of controls which are apparently strong and on which the auditor hopes to place reliance. These tests are performed on both the basic controls and the disciplines. Compliance tests include

(i)   Reperformance, which repeats in whole or in part the same work processes as performed by the company's employees,

(ii)   Examination of evidence, which consists of the inspection of records, documents and reconciliation reports for evidence that specific controls have been duly carried out,

(iii)   Observation and enquiry, to see whether certain controls are still in operation (involving interviews, spot checks and so on).

As a result of functional testing, the auditor must identify any weaknesses in the system and consider the effect these may have on his subsequent audit procedures, in particular, whether these weaknesses could lead to a material error appearing in the financial statements. If the latter possibility exists, then the auditor must alter or add to the audit procedures so that he or she can be satisfied that no material error has occurred or, if it has, assess its extent.

The last stage in the audit process is the performance of substantive tests. These are sometimes called verification procedures or validation. They are mainly concerned with verifying the existence of account balances and other information contained in the financial statements. The extent of this stage depends on the degree of reliance that can be placed on the company's internal controls. If the internal controls have proved satisfactory during the compliance tests, then the extent of the substantive tests may be limited.

Once all these stages have been completed, the auditor can express an audit opinion. In those exceptional situations where the effect of a control weakness cannot be ascertained by changes in audit procedures, or where a material error has affected the accuracy or completeness of the financial statements, the auditor will need to consider whether it may be necessary to qualify his audit report – i.e. the financial statements may not represent a true and fair view of the company.

We are now ready to see how these general concepts can be applied to computerised systems. However we will first consider the types of fraud to which computerised systems are vulnerable, and what countermeasures are possible, irrespective of the needs of the auditor.

11.3 Computer fraud

There are three main types of computer fraud

(i)   Embezzlement, whereby computer processing (either fraudulent steps in the computer program or the processing of unauthorised data) is used to defraud the company,

(ii)   Misrepresentation, whereby computer processing is used to assist in the production of financial information which is not derived from authorised transactions,

(iii)   Physical action, whereby data or programs are stolen or the computer equipment is attacked.

The main concern of the auditor is to assess whether a material error has or could arise. The perpetration of any type of fraud represents a breach in the security of a computer system. Security requires (i) that the computer is available when and only when it is required, (ii) that data is processed completely and accurately and (iii) that access to data is restricted to authorised people. The maintenance of security is usually based on a 3-pronged defence

(i)   minimise the probability of a breach in security by taking preventive action

(ii)   minimise the damage if a breach in security does occur,

(iii)   design a method for recovering from the breach in security.

As a first step, unauthorised personnel can be excluded from computer and terminal rooms by physical locks, often operated by badge keys. Once past this hurdle, access to the system itself can be protected by the allocation of authorised usernames and by a lock operated by software, namely the use of passwords. To be effective, it is important that passwords can be changed frequently, preferably by users themselves.

Further software controls, known as privacy locks or access rights, provide more precise safeguards against malicious access. Privacy locks can be applied to individuals or groups (e.g. a named employee or employees, or all members of a department) and authorise a spectrum of file operations. These include no access at all, read only, execute, append, modify or full rights, including that of amending the privacy lock itself. In some cases privacy locks can be applied to specific records or fields within a file, or to certain types of terminal or to particular application programs.

If security is breached, either accidentally or deliberately, the damage can be minimised by sensible precautions. A systematic procedure for copying files (the grandfather, father, son method) is usually adopted, with one copy being stored in a physically separate location (preferably fireproof). In addition it is standard practice to keep a journal, which logs all changes made to files, and a transaction journal (or input log). These, coupled with the previously made copies of the master files, provide a means of recovery from system failures. To avoid rerunning entire batches of data, checkpoints are built in at frequent intervals at which a 'snapshot' of the system is logged, i.e. a summary of changes which have taken place in the data since the previous checkpoint. Then if the system fails it is only necessary to reprocess the work from the last checkpoint.

Obviously 'insurance' should be taken out where possible and back-up procedures designed, e.g. ensuring that there is a suitable computer bureau to help in an emergency. If a company cannot process its sales ledger, it is unlikely that the company's customers will be honest and own up to owing money. Hence the lack of suitable physical security and back-up procedures could spell bankruptcy for the company if it lost the sales ledger and there were insufficient supporting documents to recreate it. However security costs money and therefore it is important to weigh these costs against the benefits in what is essentially a risk management exercise (see Chapter 6). The normal approach for an auditor is to weigh the odds heavily in favour of security.

11.4   Auditing in computer based systems[1]

Up to now we have discussed the main principles of auditing regardless of whether the system being audited is computerised or not. When auditing a computerised system there are basically two approaches: auditing around the computer or auditing through the computer.

Auditing around the computer is concerned with examining the input to and output from the computer, but not examining the computer's processing. This is useful in small relatively unsophisticated systems. The computer is essentially unexamined and the auditor's task is similar to that in a manual system – with the exception that some of the intermediate steps cannot be checked, so greater reliance must be placed on examining the input and output of the system.

Auditing through the computer makes use of the computer to audit itself. The auditor provides special programs and packages (sometimes referred to collectively as a *computer audit package*) to enable the computer to follow an audit trail and examine all the files concerned. A typical computer audit package could include

(i)   file interrogation programs – to examine or produce reports on master files, transaction files and temporary files,

(ii)   resident code – to examine live transactions as they are processed,

(iii)   interactive enquiry programs – to interrogate files in on-line systems,

(iv)   log analysis programs – to analyse a computer's system or console log,

(v)   comparison programs – to compare versions of a program in either source or executable form,

(vi)   flowcharting programs – to chart the logic of source programs,

(vii) test data generators – to create files of test data,

(viii) simulator programs – to simulate the processing of data through a company's accounting system using live transactions data.

These two approaches to the auditing of computer based systems express extreme situations and in practice most audits will involve a combination of both

[1] The remainder of this chapter follows the recommendations of the Institute of Chartered Accountants for England and Wales, as expressed by Jenkins and Pinkney (1979). They adopt an international approach (particularly relevant to the USA and Canada) to computer auditing; copies can be obtained from the Institute at Moorgate Place, London EC2 2BJ.

techniques. Some basic controls, particularly user controls (to be discussed below) should be the concern of the auditor whichever technique is being used. Sadly, some audits of computerised systems using the 'auditing around the computer' approach totally ignore all basic controls and disciplines over those controls. Whereas small businesses (e.g. the family butcher) will always be difficult to audit, since there are few basic controls or disciplines which can be successfully implemented, a firm of accountants has no right to apply the same lax procedures to manufacturing firms with a turnover of $10 million plus and a profit of $2 million plus.

The auditing of computer based systems follows the same broad stages as for manual systems – evaluation of internal control (i.e. basic controls and disciplines), compliance tests and substantitive tests. The general principles outlined at the beginning of this chapter still apply but the procedures which must be examined, and the methods used to examine them, are necessarily somewhat different in a computer context. In the next sections we therefore look again at these stages of the auditor's work, and describe some of the new problems and solutions which exist. We concentrate particularly on the first stage.

11.4.1 Evaluation of internal control in computer based systems
In the computer context, basic controls and disciplines can be divided into the following categories

(i)   *User controls* are manual controls carried out on the data prior to processing. These are extremely popular with firms of accountants, being easy to operate and to audit,

(ii)   *Programmed procedures* are steps inserted into computer programs in order to assist in the control of the data being processed,

(iii)   *Integrity controls* are controls over the implementation, security and use of programs, and the security of files.

An example of a user control would be a manual check that the quantity of goods despatched to a customer corresponds to the details shown on the shipping note. The proper execution of this check can be shown for audit purposes by the signature of an authorised person on one copy of the shipping note. Note that disciplines over user controls will apply to user departments as much as to the computer department. Programmed controls would include the implementation of check digits and batch totals, while integrity controls cover the full range of physical and software controls on rights of access to the computer system and the use of the information which it contains.

User controls and programmed procedures can be further subdivided in a number of ways

(i)   completeness of input and updating,

(ii)   accuracy of input and updating,

(iii)   computer generated data,

(iv)   validity of data processed,

(v)   maintenance of data on files,

(vi)   file creation.

We will consider each of these in turn.

Completeness of input and updating

An essential feature of any data processing system is that all transactions must be properly recorded, input and the relevant master files updated correctly. Whereas accuracy controls (considered in the next section) are concerned with the precision of each transaction, completeness controls are concerned with ensuring that no transactions can be overlooked.

If batch totals are used, procedures should be adopted to check that

- all documents have been placed in a batch

- all batches have been submitted

- relevant batch totals agree, or differences are investigated and corrected

- any rejected input is subsequently resubmitted

This work can be supported by the checking of printout. A printout is assessed against copies in the originating department of all documents sent for processing. The printout could also be used to check the sequence of input documents or, alternatively, to check the total number of documents.

Sequence checks can be made automatically by the computer so that all transactions entered on numbered documents are monitored. Exception reports of any missing numbers must be regularly produced and investigated, and similarly for any unmatched or mismatched items (computer matching). Where matching takes place against information stored in a master file it is important, of course, that suitable controls ensure that this basic information is itself completely and accurately maintained.

Once the input data has been accepted, there are a number of controls applied to the subsequent updating. These include the accumulation of a control total (i.e. during sequence checking or computer matching), the carrying through of control totals during intermediate processing, the reconciliation of total accepted items with an accumulation of updated records (calculated as the updating process is carried out) and the investigation and correction of differences.

Finally, since errors and uncertainties will inevitably occur, it is necessary to have detailed procedures for the prompt investigation, correction and resubmission of rejections during both the input and the update stages. Besides the need to correct the faults which led to the rejection, this check will prevent transactions from being lost as a result of falling through a rejection 'trapdoor'.

Accuracy of input and updating

Transcription errors can easily creep in during the process of transcribing information from source data to input documents, whilst conversion errors may occur when this data is converted into machine readable form. To some extent the controls discussed under 'completeness' also apply to accuracy (e.g. batch totals, checking of printouts and so on). Other checks approriate to this task have been discussed in Chapter 6, and include

format checks	dependency checks
existence checks	verification of conversion
check digit verification	security of output
reasonableness checks	

In practice an auditor will rely on a combination of the above controls.

Computer generated data

This term refers to any data which is produced as a result of calculations made by the computer system, i.e. any processing which is more than a straightforward update, for example the calculation of the discounts to be deducted for bulk orders, or the totalling of an invoice.

There are four steps which must be checked if an auditor is to be satisfied about computer generated data

(i)   the signal which triggers the generation of data must be input completely and accurately,

(ii) the process of generating the data must be logically sound,

(iii) the standing and other data on the master file (from which some of the data is generated) must be checked for completeness and accuracy,

(iv) the generated data should be manually reviewed (e.g. a scrutiny of purchase orders before dispatch) or subject to suitable programmed procedures (e.g. cheques over a certain amount reported for investigation).

Once generated the data will be subjected to the usual updating controls.

Validity of data processed

In computer systems data may be authorised prior to input, during input or after the input of transactions. In some cases the computer may be able to identify and report on items which require manual authorisation, for example excessive overtime or large tax refunds in a payroll system. In fact, the timing of authorisation may be such that the authorisation objective conflicts with the need to verify the completeness and accuracy of input. Hence unauthorised input may be acceptable provided batch totals are established and recorded, and individual items within a batch are authorised subsequently.

In the case of selective manual authorisation, the computer is programmed to identify and report on defined items by reference to a standard. The auditor should ensure that the standard is reasonable and that reported items have been duly authorised. A more complicated case of selective authorisation is programmed checking of validity where data is matched against information on another file in the system. Again control must ensure that the information on the file is complete and accurate, and that the matching process is logically sound.

Maintenance of data on files

The major purpose of maintenance controls is to reveal errors arising from the accidental corruption of data on files and to provide protection against unauthorised alterations. An effective control mechanism is the regular reconciliation of an accumulation of items on the file with an independently maintained control account; for example, a written record of the number of suppliers currently held on the suppliers file will help to detect any attempt to add fictitious names (who may then be paid for fictitious invoices!).

As computer systems become more reliable there is a decreasing risk of accidental damage to files, but measures to prevent or detect malicious changes grow steadily more important as the size and sensitivity of computer files increases.

File creation

When a new file is created during an accounting period, it will need to be checked for accuracy and completeness of the opening transaction and standing data. Whereas it may be possible to check some data with a previous file or system (e.g. opening account balances) other standing data (such as unit prices or interest rates) will not be subject to the same controls. The auditor will therefore have to satisfy himself that this data was completely and accurately input.

11.4.2 Integrity controls

Integrity controls are concerned with the basis on which a system is set up, and the manner in which it is operated, rather than with the data which the system processes. For this reason the auditor may start by considering the structure of the computer department. An auditor will be looking for a comprehensive set of integrity controls, many of which will be software based, including full disciplines as regards both the segregation of duties and supervision. In smaller computer departments the proper segregation of duties may not be possible and the auditor will not be able to place as much reliance on integrity controls (as a consequence there may be stronger user controls).

Generally speaking, the auditor will look for controls on

implementation	computer operations
cataloguing	file security
program security	

Implementation controls for new systems specify the documentation required at the system design and development stages. The need for both an outline and a detailed description was mentioned in Chapter 1, as were the various procedures (such as parallel or pilot running) which can be adopted when the new system is tested.

Cataloguing concerns the necessary procedures for introducing tested programs (new or modified) into operational use. Both manual and software controls may be used to ensure that the system as a whole remains coherent and valid as a result of the changes.

Program security controls are designed to ensure that no unauthorised changes can be made to the production programs that process data; for example, unauthorised changes to the payroll and cash payments systems are of particular concern to the auditor. The major principles are that all changes must be approved, that the actual changes are appropriate and that the changes are followed up. In general, programs should be protected by passwords so that they can be accessed only by authorised personnel. A further check, particularly if it is impossible to ensure that only authorised changes are made, is to make regular comparisons between the programs used for production runs and independently controlled copies. If programs are held off-line then they should be subject to physical library controls – securely held, issued only on appropriate authority and promptly returned.

Computer operation controls are designed to ensure that the programmed procedures which have been laid down are applied consistently during the processing of data. This includes making sure that the job control statements, run instructions and various optional parameters are checked for validity. The system software should provide no more resources than are necessary for the task in hand (e.g. no access to unnecessary files) and the system log, an automatic record of all activity during processing, can be printed out for review. The log may also be supplemented by a manual report, especially when exceptional situations occur. The auditor will usually rely on the system software to ensure that the correct files are loaded, since each file will include a header label containing the file name, date of creation and version number.

File security controls are designed to safeguard both off-line files and on-line files (whether accessed in a batch system or via terminals). A number of controls in this area have already been mentioned and are repeated here as part of the system which the auditor is responsible for verifying. For example

- the use of keys or badges to control access to terminals and/or a computer room

- passwords to authorise use of the computer system as a whole

- access rights to control which files can be used by which programs (or persons), and for what purposes (e.g. read only, append only or modify)

- a system report on attempts to violate passwords or access rights

Off-line files should be the responsibility of a file librarian and the normal precautions appropriate to valuable property should be taken against hazards such as fire and theft.

11.4.3 Compliance/functional tests

Once the evaluation of the control system has taken place, an audit plan is devised. If the evaluation indicates that reliance can be placed on the internal control system, then tests must be performed to see whether the internal control procedures comply (hence compliance) with their control objectives. In situations in which the internal control system is weak, additional substantive tests must be conducted to verify the accounts (e.g. writing to customers and suppliers to check balances).

The evaluation of the internal control system is crucially important both for the auditor and for the computer administrator. Substantive tests are expensive and one way to ensure a cheaper audit fee is to minimise the auditor's use of substantive tests. Hence the computer administrator will place great emphasis on computer controls. Assuming that proper internal controls exist, how can an auditor test that these are working correctly and justify the administrator's faith in them?

Tests of disciplines

Tests of supervisory procedures are based largely on the examination of evidence, such as authorised signatures on appropriate documents. The examination of evidence is also important when testing disciplines which involve the segregation of duties or custodial controls, but in these cases rather greater emphasis is laid on observation and enquiry, for example, employees may be asked what they understand their duties and responsibilities to be.

Tests of user controls and programmed procedures
Many controls in this area, such as batch totals, validation procedures or file access, can be tested by the examination of evidence and by reperformance. In the latter case it will usually be sufficient to test just a sample of batches of data, or a random period of on-line input, but a major problem occurs if it is not possible to follow the audit trail (for example, if totals and reports are printed without supporting details).

There are four types of tests which can be made

(i) manual tests on programmed procedures can be performed when there is full visible evidence available – for example, a sales total where a complete listing of sales invoices is provided,

(ii) audit test data – this is submitted to and processed by a company's operational procedures, so that the resulting output can be checked against predicted results,

(iii) program code analysis – this is undertaken by the auditor, who examines source listings of operational programs to ensure that all the relevant procedures (including control procedures) are present and are logically coded,

(iv) simulation – the routine daily transactions of a company are processed by programs provided by the auditor and the results compared with those produced by the company's system. The comparison may be made by a special audit program which can print a report on the differences which it detects (see Fig. 11.1).

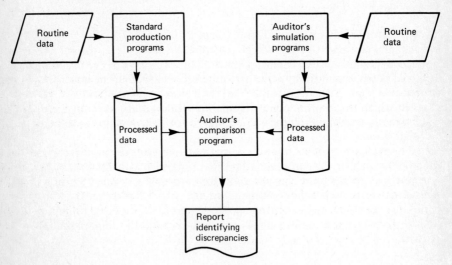

Fig. 11.1 Use of simulation programs in functional testing

Tests of integrity controls
All three modes of functional testing are likely to be used here – re-performance, examination of evidence, and observation/enquiry (p. 210). The tests which are carried out should include a sample of the systems software and, as for simulation, special computer programs can help in this task, for example, programs

which analyse and report on the system log and programs which will compare the production software with independently controlled copies which are alleged to be identical. By noting any discrepancies in the latter case the auditor can check whether all authorised changes, and no others, have been properly implemented.

Compliance testing is often a time consuming process and an auditor may try to use some other method to ascertain whether a particular internal control procedure is working satisfactorily. These alternatives could involve some substantive tests, in the form of computer programs to examine large volumes of processed data, or relying on controls provided by programmed procedures and the systems software. However, these approaches are vulnerable if systems designers fail to include adequate control measures or fail to ensure that the measures provided are enforced at all times.

11.4.4   Substantive tests

An example of a substantive test is the examination of a batch of invoices to make sure that the invoices were posted in the correct period and to the correct sales ledger accounts. More generally, substantive tests may include

- confirmation – verification of a fact or condition from a third party

- inspection – counting or examining physical objects represented by items in the accounts

- reperformance – e.g. the recalculation/computation/accumulation of an account balance

- vouching – the examination of evidence supporting or authorising a transaction or item in order to determine its validity

To aid the auditor in implementing substantive tests, two techniques are used: (i) reconciliation (e.g. the total of sales ledger accounts with the debtors control account, or the cash account in the general ledger with the bank statements) and (ii) account analysis, which involves summarising or categorising the details of an account in order to provide a better understanding of the items comprising the balance. Auditors make use of special file interrogation programs to help them with these tasks.

An extended substantive test which is made by auditors is the use of *resident* or *embedded code*. This consists of program steps written by the auditor and inserted into the company's production programs with the objective of reviewing live transactions as they are processed. Fig. 11.2 illustrates the use of this technique. Two types of audit files may be created: (i) a file of all items passing or failing particular tests specified in the resident code and (ii) a file of a random sample of all items passing through the resident code.

11.5   Auditing and computer administration

As we have seen, one aspect of an external audit will be an evaluation of the entire internal control system for a company's accounting, including computer controls. Subsequently the auditor is required to report to senior management any material weaknesses in the internal control system. It will then be the duty of the computer manager, or some other senior computer administrator, to

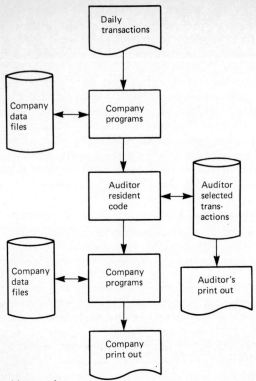

Fig. 11.2 Use of resident code

discuss the feasibility and cost of improving any computer controls where weaknesses have been noted.

As discussed in Chapter 6, a guarantee of absolute control is impossible and to some extent there is bound to be a conflict of objectives between the auditor and the computer administrator. The auditor is concerned with gaining evidence to support an opinion on the financial statements, whilst the computer administrator is attempting to provide the maximum information for the minimum cost. Each must understand the other's position. There have certainly been instances when the auditor would have liked to improve the internal control system but such improvements have been overruled by top management as being insufficiently cost-effective. However, a failure to co-operate may lead to the withholding or qualification of an audit opinion.

The auditor should acknowledge that a good computer administrator will, in his own interests, include as many controls in the system as he feels he can reasonably justify. Conversely the computer administrator should recognise that the work of the auditor can help to identify weaknesses in the computer controls which are currently in use. It will usually be much cheaper to correct these faults at an early stage than to proceed in blissful ignorance until major damage occurs in the form of a serious fraud or loss of information.

The auditor's viewpoint is in one sense broader than the computer administrator's since he is concerned with the origins of transactions, which include manual processing procedures and not just controls in the computer environment. On the other hand he is interested only in the validity of the financial reports which are produced and not in such questions as the efficiency of the computer service or the type of system which it offers to its users. What both men have in common is a determination to ensure that the computer system runs correctly and securely.

11.6 Auditing specialised computer systems

11.6.1 On-line systems
Some of the more advanced computer systems create new problems for the auditor. The expansion of on-line data entry systems has caused particular concern since some conventional controls, such as batching, control totals and balancing, may no longer be appropriate.

In these cases great care and attention must be given to the checks on accuracy which are made when data is input. These checks are summarised in Table 11.1 and use whatever information is available in the system to analyse the consistency and reliability of the input data (see also Martin, 1973b).

There are important implications for analysts, designers and administrators. An on-line system must be designed to catch as many errors as possible immediately on input; any errors so caught must be immediately corrected; self checking operations should be built into the terminal dialogue with the user and the linkage of this dialogue to file inspection routines.

Furthermore, control is improved when the real-time error detection process is backed up by off-line file inspection and balancing routines. Consequently systems analysts must play an active part in the design of controls in computer systems, even if some of these may fall in users' areas, and computer administrators must give close attention to the quality of the manual and administrative controls which surround and protect the on-line computer controls.

11.6.2 Mini and micro computer systems
For many minicomputer systems emphasis can be placed on the same controls and procedures as for larger systems. The same cannot be said of all

Table 11.1   On-line and real-time accuracy checks

Single transaction checks	Group transaction checks
Descriptive read back	Periodic item balances
Character and field checks	Running totals
Links to earlier transactions	Checkpoints at which the operator must inspect the input or status of the entry and verify that it is correct
Check for a valid sequence of transactions	
Use of machine-readable documents	
Check for internal contradictions	
Check that all facts have been entered	

microprocessor based business systems and small minicomputer systems. In these situations there is usually no segregation of duties: programming, operational and managerial functions may be combined and, for example, this makes it much easier to effect unauthorised changes. To detect such changes would place an extra workload on the auditor (e.g. taking copies of source programs and periodically checking the current version against the original). A further problem is that some of the software for small systems – often sold at the bottom end of the price range – is unreliable and does not have all the usual computer based controls built-in.

What can be done about these cheap systems? They do not occur only in small businesses, since large businesses are also buying them for use in a network as a cheaper alternative to a large centralised mainframe computer.

The first principle to remember is that these are on-line systems and, therefore, despite the extra expense, it is vitally important that all the appropriate on-line controls are incorporated into the system and its business environment.

A second important point is that an accurate record of all input and output will be required. This means ensuring

(i)   that input is logged on to a printer (the program should stop 'gracefully' if the printer goes off-line),

(ii)   that a copy of all output (i.e. 2-part paper) is maintained for inspection.

A third principle is to enforce security copying – the system should ask the user to copy his or her files on closedown or startup.

Once these precautions have been taken the most important feature that an auditor will look for is the presence of a strong and clear audit trail – for example, each account balance should be traceable back to the relevant transactions and vice versa.

11.6.3 Data base systems

One important way in which data bases differ from conventional systems is the nature of the data itself: in principle it is held only once, with several applications sharing the same stored data items. This implies that the traditional responsibility of each user for the integrity of his own files disappears. To fill this vacuum, responsibility for data in a data base is transferred to a data base administrator (DBA), as we saw in Chapter 10.

So far so good, but the DBA does not satisfy the segregation principle: he has the knowledge, opportunity and authority to access the data and perpetrate accidental or deliberate errors. A general solution to the power and authority of the DBA lies in his responsibility to the user departments. Since they are vitally interested in the accuracy of the data, this provides a form of control somewhat similar to that exerted on a company by its customers, who are more than ready to question any erroneous or dubious statements which they receive.

Another control problem in data base systems is the authorisation of input once data becomes 'public property' (recall the phrase *a central resource* in Chapter 10). The principle usually adopted is to delegate the DBA's overall authority to some specific department or group for each area of data. This department must then accept both the responsibility for controlling new data in this area and also the obligation to make 'its' stored data available to all authorised users. In practice these checks will be exercised by suitable parts of the data base system software over which the DBA and his agents (and they alone) will have control.

Most auditors will look increasingly to the data base software, as supplied by the computer manufacturer or software house, to maintain controls on the integrity and security of a data base system. Some of the ways in which this can be done were discussed in Chapter 10. The auditor will supplement these controls by checks to ensure that the data base software has not been altered.

11.7 Conclusion

Auditing is a collection of tools and procedures that together form a coherent whole. The auditor must be satisfied as to the extent of his audit tests, but different situations and circumstances may lead to different tests and procedures being used, and each accounting firm has its own view of which tests are appropriate and reliable. An accounting firm may be sued for negligence so the auditor will always attempt to place reliance only on those tests which, in the firm's experience, have proved satisfactory. Since the more sophisticated computer systems are a relatively recent innovation, the experience of firms is constantly being updated and modified. Older batch processing systems were readily amenable to user controls, and tests of disciplines over user controls, but with online and real-time systems, file security and program security controls become more important. Nevertheless the major emphasis in the auditing of computer based systems still appears to be to place reliance on tests of user controls and programmed procedures.

It is difficult to arrange auditing procedures in a precise structure, since auditing is an art that places a significant emphasis on judgement. Information systems are enormously diverse and varied and the auditor could spend vast sums of money on various auditing tests. The art of auditing is to use only those resources which yield a degree of confidence that there is no material error. Almost every information system is different, so the actual tests used will vary not only from system to system but also with the firm and maybe even with the auditing personnel assigned to that system. If, during the process of the audit, a weakness or possible error is discovered then this may change the whole course of the audit. Therefore the audit process is also dependent on the results of the tests and these may vary on each occasion.

In some ways, the whole auditing procedure may seem something of a waste of time. However, external auditing is a legal requirement and a qualified auditor's report, in which the external auditor cannot say that the accounts are a true and fair view of the business, may have severe ramifications for a business; for example, providers of finance may not be so willing to lend money if the auditors feel unable to give the accounts of a company a clean bill of health! There is another important purpose behind both internal and external auditing. The fact that such auditing procedures exist and are an ongoing process does exert a deterrent effect on dishonest or potentially dishonest personnel. Indeed, from the management point of view the deterrent effect of auditing may be of more importance than the possibility of actually discovering frauds.

Many smaller accounting firms still concentrate on auditing around the computer. However, with expertise becoming more widespread and a larger number of clients becoming computerised, auditing of computer based systems is relying to a greater extent on auditing through the computer. The impact on the computer scientist is twofold. Firstly, he or she can no longer design commercial computer systems without reference to auditing considerations. Secondly, computer scientists may be called upon to help design and implement the array of computer programs listed on page 212. As the computer based systems become increasingly complex, involving data communications, data bases, automatic data capture and distributed processing networks, so the range and extent of auditing problems will increase.

In the long run there can be little doubt that auditing considerations will dictate the design of future systems rather than be a consideration once a system is up and running. Thus it is vital for those who are designing systems to be fully aware of the precise nature and requirements of auditing. To design a system without taking auditing into account, and then to build in auditing links and routines, may be an inefficiency that the computing and business world can no longer afford.

Questions

11.1 What are the two general approaches to the auditing of computer based systems? Illustrate each approach with a number of examples.

11.2 Describe some accidental or deliberate errors which are less likely in a computerised than a manual system.

11.3 What is the importance of an audit trail? Is its existence more critical for a small business system? What is the importance of organisational structure on internal control in larger organisations?

11.4 A building society has an on-line real-time computer system. Each clerk at the head office and at the 50 branch offices has an on-line input/output terminal similar to an automated bank telling machine, but one which also prints on the customer's passbook. A customer's savings account deposits and withdrawals are recorded by a clerk at the time of each transaction. The accounting and EDP departments are centred at the head office where mortgage payments are processed in batch mode.

Identify the controls which should be in effect in such a system.

11.5 A company's files are a valuable source of information. Explain the steps which might be taken to safeguard the files against

(a) power failure,   (b) fire,

(c) vandalism,   (d) software errors,

(e) hardware errors,   (f) accidental errors by a terminal operator,

(g) conspiracy between a programmer and an operator,

(h) a terminal operator who was allowed to record all data on a purchase ledger and who had set up a bogus company which had supplied non-existent goods,

(i) an owner of a small business who wished to defraud the company in an attempt to pay less tax.

Further business applications

12.1 Extended sales systems

In Chapter 7 we saw how a minimal computer based sales system would involve just the sales ledger (i.e. the subsidiary accounts receivable system). Basically a minimal system would allow the input of invoices, cash receipts, adjustments and various standing data amendments. Using the two master files (customer file and transaction file), plus various other parameter and control files, it is possible to produce the necessary major reports, such as customer statements, age of debt report and so on. However, there are a number of possible extensions to this system, which fall into three major categories: sales or marketing analysis, order processing and inventory control.

12.1.1 Sales analysis

The aim of this important function is to summarise and compare information about sales under various categories and for various time periods, e.g. sales by product group, by region, by salesman, by type of customer. This can be done by adding appropriate codes to each sales transaction (i.e. invoice). The customer file also contains relevant information, such as volume data and other sales this month or in previous months. There is usually a sales analysis file which is updated after a transaction has taken place (Fig. 12.1). The analyses produced in this way help a business to estimate future sales and formulate a suitable

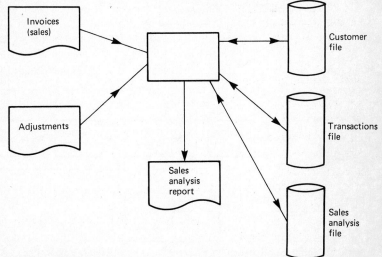

Fig. 12.1 Sales Analysis

product/market strategy (i.e. what are the best goods to produce and what are the best areas of the market at which to aim?).

12.1.2 Order entry and processing
Orders which are to be put into the system are first checked to see whether the goods are in stock (with some remedial action if they are not, such as 'raising' a back-order) and whether the new order exceeds the customer's credit limit. If both conditions are satisfied, an entry can be created in the order file. After this the job involves monitoring the progress of an order, keeping control of any incomplete orders and issuing manufacturing instructions if necessary. Order processing may also include the production of a picking list (i.e. a list of which goods to 'pick' out of the warehouse). Finally delivery notes will be produced and form a basis for invoices.

12.1.3 Finished goods inventory control
A finished goods stock file may be updated simultaneously with the creation of an invoice. The invoice may be priced by reference to sales prices held on the stock file. Possible extra reports include an invoice run and a stock issue report.

An expanded sales system will naturally impinge on other areas of a business. For example, Fig. 12.2 shows an overview of a computer system for a retail store. In this case the overall system has been subdivided into a sales system, an associated receipts and disbursement system, and a financial accounting and control system. The store is assumed to have a large volume hi-fi business, with cash and credit customers who may place orders by mail, by telephone or in person. Fig. 12.2 shows in outline how the subsystems interrelate and the individual parts are shown in more detail in Fig. 12.3(a)–(h), which are self-explanatory.

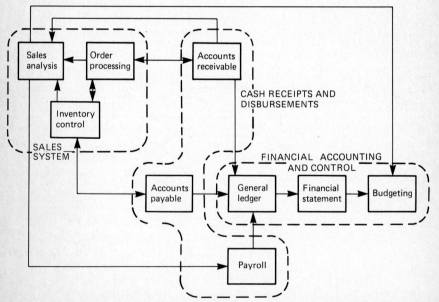

Fig. 12.2 Communication between subsystems in a retail system (*From* Page & Hooper, 1979)

12.2 Financial information systems

A study of Fig. 12.2 reveals one of the classic European and US accounting conventions: that the financial aspects of an information system are segregated into two distinct subsystems: one dealing with cash receipts and cash payments – the so-called cash receipts and disbursement system; and another dealing with the general ledger, the production of financial reports and the budgeting system – the general ledger system or financial accounting and control system.

The cash receipts and disbursement system includes accounts receivable (sales ledger), accounts payable (purchase ledger) and payroll subsystems (see also Chapter 4).

The budgeting system is the heart of the financial control system. An organisation's performance against its budget or plan is regularly monitored (say, monthly) with variances and actual values reported back to those who have responsibility for each area of the business. The vital nature of a business control system was discussed in Chapter 3, and most organisations place a heavy reliance on the budgeting system for this purpose.

Fig. 12.4 shows another example of a computer based information system in which these financial subsystems can be seen. In this example the sales subsystem has been referred to as marketing but the three major components can nevertheless be observed: sales/marketing analysis, order processing and finished goods inventory control. (Other arrangements of these subsystems are also possible, for example, the accounts receivable (sales ledger) system could be operated within the sales section). Notice that this example also includes a collection of subsystems which form production (or manufacturing) subsystems. We shall discuss these shortly.

12.2.1 Costing systems

Each cost posted to a general ledger subsystem may be allocated to a manufacturing plant, a division, a parent company, a region or some other group. In Chapter 3 the term responsibility accounting was introduced. This simply means that reports are sent to a manager who is responsible for all revenues, costs and other important statistics concerning his or her area of control (see p. 32).

In reporting revenues and costs, there are important principles at stake. For example, how much should a sales manager be charged towards the costs of running the computer centre? Of course the first job is to determine what the costs of running the computer centre are. As systems become more complex, cost collection and recording schemes become more important, and there is a vast area of accounting, known as cost accounting, which lays down the theory through which labour, raw material and overhead costs can be collected. At the risk of over-simplifying the problem, there are two basic methods of organising cost collection schemes

(i)   *Job costing* – all costs are collected by a particular job number (which may be either an order for a customer or replenishments of warehouse stocks of a standard product). Labour and raw material costs (sometimes called direct costs) can be identified fairly easily with individual jobs. Overheads (such as the foreman's wage, fork truck costs, office expenses) must be allocated to various jobs in some systematic way,

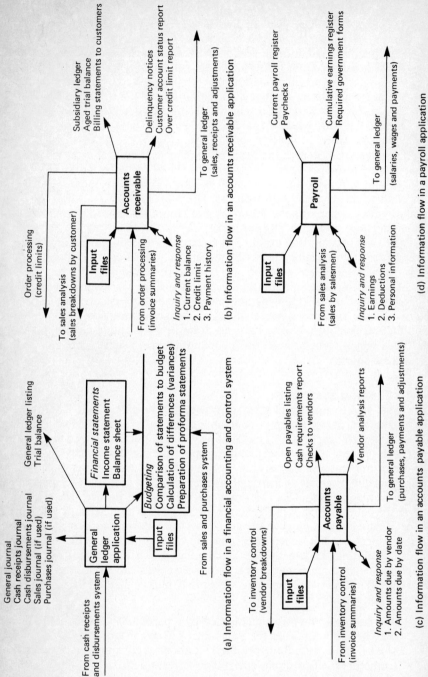

Subsidiary ledger
Aged trial balance
Billing statements to customers

Delinquency notices
Customer account status report
Over credit limit report

Order processing
(credit limits)

To sales analysis
(sales breakdowns by customer)

Accounts receivable

Input files

From order processing
(invoice summaries)

Inquiry and response
1. Current balance
2. Credit limit
3. Payment history

To general ledger
(sales, receipts and adjustments)

(b) Information flow in an accounts receivable application

Current payroll register
Paychecks

Cumulative earnings register
Required government forms

Payroll

Input files

From sales analysis
(sales by salesmen)

Inquiry and response
1. Earnings
2. Deductions
3. Personal information

To general ledger
(salaries, wages and payments)

(d) Information flow in a payroll application

General ledger listing
Trial balance

Financial statements
Income statement
Balance sheet

Budgeting
Comparison of statements to budget
Calculation of differences (variances)
Preparation of proforma statements

General journal
Cash receipts journal
Cash disbursements journal
Sales journal (if used)
Purchases journal (if used)

General ledger application

Input files

From cash receipts
and disbursements system

From sales and purchases system

(a) Information flow in a financial accounting and control system

Open payables listing
Cash requirements report
Checks to vendors

Vendor analysis reports

To inventory control
(vendor breakdowns)

Accounts payable

Input files

From inventory control
(invoice summaries)

Inquiry and response
1. Amounts due by vendor
2. Amounts due by date

To general ledger
(purchases, payments and adjustments)

(c) Information flow in an accounts payable application

Fig. 12.3 (From Page & Hooper, 1979)

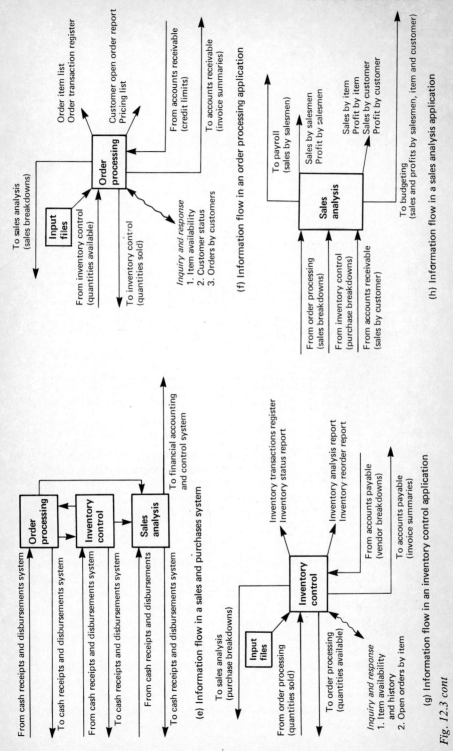

(e) Information flow in a sales and purchases system

(f) Information flow in an order processing application

(g) Information flow in an inventory control application

(h) Information flow in a sales analysis application

Fig. 12.3 cont

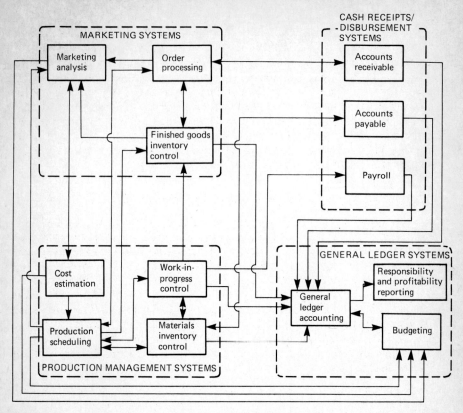

Fig. 12.4 An overview of a computer-based information system

(ii)   *Process costing* – instead of costs being allocated to a particular job, some manufacturing environments (e.g. oil refineries) find it more meaningful to collect together costs relating to a particular process, assembly technique or production line. Once again, indirect and overhead costs have to be allocated in some systematic way.

There are also two fundamental approaches to the allocation of costs. The first (called absorption costing) allocates all fixed overheads such as rent and administrative costs as a charge on products, whilst the second method (direct or marginal costing) accepts fixed overheads as a central charge on the organisation and allocates to products only those costs which are directly incurred in manufacture, such as raw material, energy and labour costs.

One further costing concept that is important in all environments is that of a *cost centre*. Whether process or job costing is being carried out costs are usually collected 'by cost centre', i.e. some boundary is drawn round a part of the organisation and all direct costs are recorded for that cost centre. Often there may be a hierarchical structure to cost centres: several cost centres may make up an operating unit and several operating units may make a regional cost centre and so on. Cost centres may also have their costs subdivided by product, process or job. Thus a wide range of questions may be asked by management; for example, find out all direct labour costs, in cost centres X, Y, and Z, attributable to product A or process B. Alternatively, how many of part N were used throughout Europe in the production of product Y in assembly process P during the last three years (broken down by month and by cost centre) and if possible identify the suppliers and the volumes supplied.

The first question may have been asked with the objective of trying to improve productivity, to examine the financial wisdom of greater automation or to examine the consequences of a strike. The second question may be geared to searching for bulk buying discounts, a search for new suppliers in certain areas, the redesign of the part or so forth. The solution to both questions requires a data base approach, as discussed in Chapter 10.

12.3　Manufacturing/production systems

As Fig. 12.4 suggests, a manufacturing system is usually somewhat more complicated than a retail system. At least two stock control systems are needed, one for raw materials and one for finished goods, while work-in-progress (i.e. partly finished manufactured items) represents a third distinct area where rapidly changing stock should be monitored. Customers will often require an estimate of costs before placing an order and so the raw material, machine time and labour resources which will be necessary must be analysed and costed. When orders are confirmed they must be translated into production schedules, which may mean ordering more raw materials (this too must be monitored and controlled) or acquiring extra labour and/or equipment. The objectives of a production schedule include

- maximum manufacturing throughput

- maximum machine utilisation

- minimum work-in-progress

- special facilities for high priority orders

A good scheduling system will attempt to produce an optimal production plan which meets these objectives.

Fig. 12.5 demonstrates in more detail the larger set of transactions which are associated with a manufacturing environment, but even this diagram does not represent an exhaustive list.

12.4　Other routine applications

Some other routine but specialised company activities provide further scope for computer based data processing. Two such examples are

(i)　the Fixed Asset register – this maintains information about the fixed assets of a company, such as purchase price, current cost, depreciation provisions and relevant price indices (such as rebuilding costs). There is usually some form of link between this register and the general ledger system,

(ii)　the Share register – this contains the names and addresses of shareholders and the size of their shareholdings. It is used for routine correspondence, such as the annual report or new equity issues, or when paying dividends.

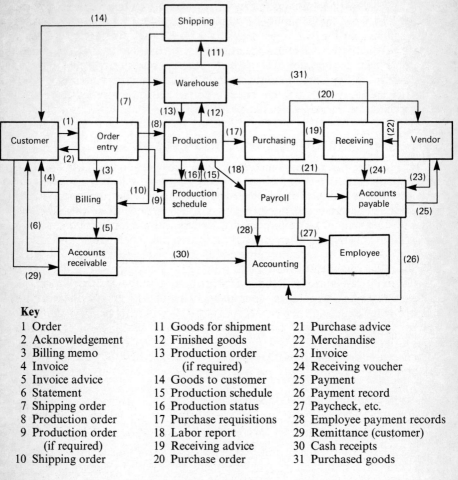

Key

1 Order	11 Goods for shipment	21 Purchase advice
2 Acknowledgement	12 Finished goods	22 Merchandise
3 Billing memo	13 Production order	23 Invoice
4 Invoice	(if required)	24 Receiving voucher
5 Invoice advice	14 Goods to customer	25 Payment
6 Statement	15 Production schedule	26 Payment record
7 Shipping order	16 Production status	27 Paycheck, etc.
8 Production order	17 Purchase requisitions	28 Employee payment records
9 Production order	18 Labor report	29 Remittance (customer)
(if required)	19 Receiving advice	30 Cash receipts
10 Shipping order	20 Purchase order	31 Purchased goods

Fig. 12.5 Transaction flow in a manufacturing firm

12.5 Developments in real-time systems

Many of the systems described in this chapter may be quite complex but all of those discussed so far use conventional, well established technology. However, major new developments in data communication techniques are now being closely integrated with progress in computer technology. These important changes will undoubtedly create new business methods and opportunities and will radically alter the business environment. Some of the possible developments are mentioned below.

12.5.1 Electronic invoicing

A computer produced invoice would be prepared in the usual way, but instead of being printed and mailed it would be transmitted directly to the computer system of the customer. Unique identifying numbers for the transmitting and receiving organisations would be essential, as well as the normal invoice number, and a standard protocol would have to be agreed. When the invoice had been received and understood, the receiving computer system might send a message back to the transmitting computer saying 'invoice received and understood' (but not necessarily authorised for payment; this would occur at a later stage). If a breakdown occurred in either computer system or in the data transmission system, then the sending computer would continue to send the invoice until it was correctly received; if the invoice was received but did not make sense, then the receiving computer could ask for clarification or ask for the whole invoice to be sent again.

12.5.2 Electronic ordering
If electronic invoicing is taken one stage further back, then ordering may also be carried out electronically.

The same types of procedures would be undertaken in a manual or electronic ordering system as in the invoicing system, with one exception. If an order cannot be completed or can only be part-fulfilled, then a much more sophisticated reply system would be necessary.

12.5.3 Electronic payment
Already payroll tapes are passed to banks and security firms for crediting employee's bank accounts and making up payroll packets. It will not be long before electronic cancelling of mutual debt through contra payments will be undertaken automatically. (When firm A owes $100 to firm B and firm B owes $75 to firm A, a *contra* payment by firm B to firm A of $75 would leave firm A only owing $25 to firm B.) However, this step will be overshadowed by the development in electronic payment mentioned below.

12.5.4 Electronic funds transfer system
Electronic funds transfer (EFTS) will permit the widespread use of *electronic money* between individuals and organisations, rendering the current system of cheques, pay-in books and credit cards redundant.

An EFTS system would involve EFTS stations or *automated teller machines* that could be situated in banks and connected to point-of-sale equipment at shops. All stations would be capable of debiting and crediting bank accounts. Some stations would also be able to receive and dispense cash. The updating of bank accounts would involve an EFTS card, similar to current credit cards but probably with a magnetically encoded strip of material (to supply the computer with the account number), and will let the card holder choose which account to credit. Thus automatic teller machines in an EFTS placed in a bank could be used to

- make a deposit to one's own account
- withdraw cash
- transfer cash electronically from one's own account to the account of a creditor
- enquire about the balance in one's own account

A combined point-of-sale/EFTS terminal in a retail store would provide further functions. Fig. 12.6 shows how the retail store's accounting, sales analysis and stock control updating, together with the banking transactions, can all be performed by means of one wave of a wand over the bar code on the goods, together with the insertion of a customer's EFTS card.

12.5.5 Electronic mail

The use of electronic invoices, ordering and payment systems will reduce the burden on the postal service. With new and improved data communications resources, sending other information will also be faster and cheaper than the current postal service. The transmission of letters and facsimile images (i.e. signatures, diagrams and photographs) will take only a few seconds. Routine letters can simply be typed by the receiver's computer. Letters requiring signatures can either be typed with a password (known to the receiver) or through the use of facsimile image printers.

12.5.6 The electronic office

Word processing facilities are already becoming familiar in many offices. The powerful features available include the addition or deletion of text at any specified point in a stored document, pagination, paragraphing, headings, mar-

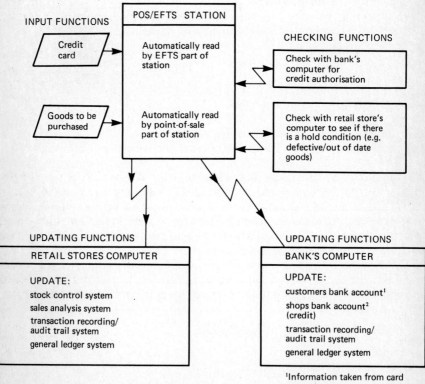

Fig. 12.6 A cash sale using a point-of-sale and an electronic funds transfer system

gins and other format control, and the incorporation of standard letters or paragraphs in new documents. All of these features can be provided either by simple 'stand-alone' systems dedicated to word processing, or as part of the facilities of a large general-purpose computer system.

However the real power of this new technology will be realised as word processing facilities are merged with the computing and data communication functions. All paper files could be stored in a company-wide electronic mail and message system that could provide immediate delivery of words and pictures, together with the interrogation of the firm's data processing files. Furthermore, input to the computer system may be possible in the future either by a keyboard, by a letter or by the spoken voice. There is therefore no distinction between mail and a telephone call. Such an electronic mail and message system might provide the following functions

(i)   a message distribution service with messages delivered to specified individuals or identified groups,

(ii)   a message reception service which can automatically receive or hold messages, redirect them if necessary and possibly operate a priority algorithm to select the most important messages to be transmitted onwards,

(iii) a computerised conference facility. Since all conference material may be stored (dialogue as well as papers), a person may sit down at a terminal at any convenient time, call up unseen conversations or papers, make additional comments and respond to questions.

Although it is difficult to be sure of the timescale, there is little doubt that some of these developments will be used within the next ten years or so – particularly the electronic funds transfer system. Of course the changes will not appear overnight, nor will every business take part, but the possibilities which have been described show the potential which real-time computing systems and electronics still have to offer.

12.6   Predictive applications

Many of the applications discussed in this book are backward looking or historical – that is, information is collected about past events or events currently taking place. Thus the information relayed to management concerns past historical data. But computers are increasingly being used to provide management with information about future events by various forecasts and projections. This is sometimes called a decision support role.

One of the most popular types of computer application is the financial model, sometimes known as the corporate model. This category of model is deterministic (i.e. single point rather than probabilistic estimates) and simulates a company over time.

The purpose of a simulation model is to simulate the activity of a company over a given time span or model horizon (e.g. 5 years). During this time it will use a set of assumptions embodied in the input data and, by applying certain formulae, will produce a set of results for each year which form the output of the model. Fig. 12.7 shows how some input may only be required initially (such as the opening bank balance) whilst other information (such as sales forecasts) will be required for each time period.

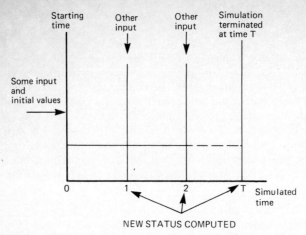

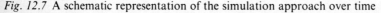

NEW STATUS COMPUTED

Fig. 12.7 A schematic representation of the simulation approach over time

The technical term which is used to describe various financial and physical terms is a variable. A variable in terms of a mathematical model is an item which is uniquely represented. The simplest example of a model is

$$R = P \times Q$$
(revenue = price multiplied by quantity)

The variables of this mathematical model are R, P and Q. In order to determine the output (R), input data is required for P and Q. The technical term for variables whose values are taken from input data is *exogenous* – that is, determined outside the model. Those variables whose values are calculated within a model are termed *endogenous* variables. The relationships which transform the exogenous variables (inputs) into values for endogenous variables (output) are termed functional relationships. An example of a functional relationship linking price and quantity to revenue is given above.

12.6.1 Econometric approach

One type of model which may be constructed attempts to represent the causal relationships in a company or environment. For example, demand for consumer durables may be functionally related to gross national product, per capita real income, credit restrictions and so forth. If the coefficients measuring the effect of these components on demand can be statistically estimated then, by specifying future values for these variables, a forecast for demand can be made – as shown in Fig. 12.8. The disadvantages of this technique are: (i) it requires specialist knowledge to create the model and estimate its coefficients; and (ii) forecasts of the causal variables must be made in order to determine the future value of the variable in which we are interested. Thus instead of estimating one variable, the modeller may have to estimate several, intuitively or otherwise. This technique is theoretically the most appealing. So as to catch the simultaneous movement of several causal variables, it may be necessary to estimate what is known as a *simultaneous equations* model. Such models require even more specialist skills and the simpler but theoretically inferior techniques may be easier to use for the financial modeller.

METHOD OF OBTAINING EXOGENOUS INPUT DATA

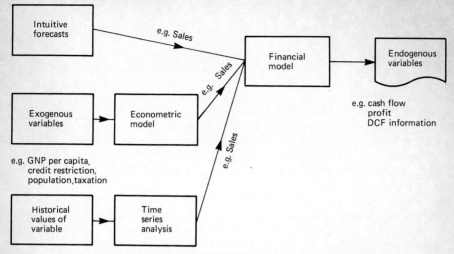

Fig. 12.8 Forecasting methods for determining input data of exogenous variables in a financial model

12.6.2 Time series analysis

The second broad classification of statistical models differs from the superior econometric approach in that only historical values of the variables to be forecast are necessary in deriving a value of an input variable to the financial model – as shown in Fig. 12.8. The theory assumes that a time series is made up of a number of components: an absolute level, a trend from this level, a seasonal pattern (there may be several, e.g. monthly, summer/winter, business cycles, etc.) and a random disturbance term. Various techniques are used to attempt to decompose these constituents of a time series and, by using the decomposed information, to derive forecasts. Within this broad category of statistical models, there are a variety of distinct techniques, e.g.

- trend lines and curves
- moving averages
- exponential smoothing
- multiplicative or additive smoothing
- adaptive methods of exponential smoothing (e.g. Trigg's tracking method)
- autoregressive techniques
- Box-Jenkins (a mixture of autoregressive and moving averages)
- multivariate Box-Jenkins techniques

Box-Jenkins is probably considered the most sophisticated of these techniques, although autoregressive methods are almost as good and are simpler for the modeller to use.

Time series analysis is less appropriate for forecasting applications such as predicting the rate of inflation. A simple econometric model with an appropriate lag structure of the form, say

$$\text{inflation rate}_t = f(\text{unemployment}_t, \text{consumption}_{t-1}, \text{money supply}_{t-2})$$

may be better, whilst purists would argue that nothing less than a full blown simultaneous equations macro-economic model would be sufficient to forecast the rate of inflation accurately. The range of applications to which planning models can be put are: short term budgeting to long term planning (including strategic models), statistical forecasting models, marketing models, capital budgeting models, acquisition models, optimising models, cash flow forecasting models and control functions. These independent planning functions are often carried out in total isolation; a more rational framework would attempt to integrate the three main planning functions of decision making, forecasting in its wider sense, and control.

With the advances in the use of data bases and their management, routine accounting information (such as the sales ledger/accounts receivable file, purchase ledger/accounts payable and other standard accounting information) could be held on a data base. Company policy decisions, including new capital expenditures already committed, product/market strategic decisions, union agreements and plans, would also be held on a file as in Fig. 12.9. Intuitive forecasts, and statistical forecasting models using historical information contained in the data base, will provide a central range (not one unique range but several alternatives) of forecasts, plans and assumptions pertaining to the exogenous variables. A financial simulation model can then translate the assumptions file into a range of endogenous variables to make a forecast file. At any one time the company may have a best estimate, but this will change frequently in response to new information. If optimising models are used they too ought to be included in this planning process.

The routine accounting information will be updated regularly. As the data

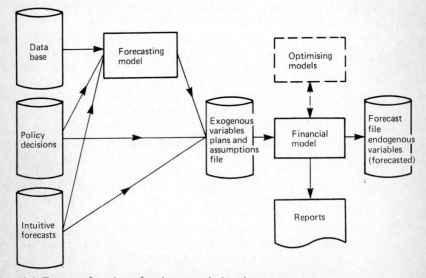

Fig. 12.9 Forecast function of an integrated planning system

base is updated this allows the continuous monitoring of the performance of the company. By feeding in factors outside the control of the company (external variances), and by rerunning the financial model with these changed plans, a more detailed variance analysis can be evolved. It may also become necessary to revise the best estimates, which may mean the reversal of some previous decisions.

12.7 Information and managerial needs

Earlier in the book we discussed the importance of information in running a business. Better information should result in good decisions, which stem from more skilled management, which will in turn result in the successful achievement of targets and goals.

Information can be either internal or external. Internal information is gained through routine data processing of internal documents (and external documents that are assimilated as internal ones); for example, new information is generated from the processing of current transactions together with stored information relating to past transactions.

External or environmental data is that which is collected other than by routine data processing on relevant topics, such as customers, suppliers, competitors, technology, the economy, government and changing patterns of demand. Both types of data are important, though different levels of management require different types of information. The information system must deliver the relevant and correct amount of information at the appropriate time. Higher levels of management will spend a greater proportion of their time in planning activities. As a consequence they will require summarised internal information but will depend more heavily on external and environmental information (see Fig. 12.10). Lower levels of management will spend a greater proportion of their time in control activities and hence require detailed internal information.

Traditional information systems may not be able to provide different managerial levels with the appropriate information. However, the new developments in computer hardware and software can satisfy the need for better management information by being more selective. The developments discussed in this book can lead to advanced management information systems which provide better managerial information – the system should be able to tailor the information to the needs of the management at all levels.

An accounting system, which stores a minimal sales and purchase system, a comprehensive chart of accounts and a consequent general ledger system, is not sufficient to provide accurate, timely, complete, concise and relevant information (the desirable properties of a management information system). Extra information such as volume or quantity data, pricing information and historical information are all required. More importantly this data may need to be broken down and associated in new ways. The user's view of data may be entirely different from the way in which the data was input to the system; for example, an order may be viewed as a number of orders for a customer, a number of orders for a product, or a number of orders requiring the same raw materials or parts. These distinct multiple views require the use of sophisticated software as described in Chapter 10. Such modern data bases are still in their infancy but they allow the possibility of providing a more advanced information system for management which, with proper use, will lead to better decisions being made.

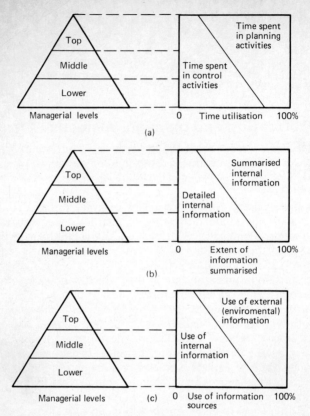

Fig. 12.10 Different managerial levels require different information (*From* Sanders, 1979)

Questions

12.1 Explain the interactions between the following subsystems

order processing   sales ledger   general ledger
inventory control   purchase ledger   payroll
sales analysis

12.2 Fig. 12.2 shows three application areas. Suggest two other ways in which the components may be divided into three application areas.

12.3 What are the distinguishing characteristics of a retail and a manufacturing information system?

12.4 Much of the data contained in an information system is historical. Is this always true and what are the advantages of a forward-looking system?

12.5 Financial simulation models are equivalent to 'crystal-ball gazing'. Discuss.

12.6 Provide examples of complex enquiries, necessitating a data base, which might be asked by differing levels of management.

Bibliography

Abramson, N. 1963. *Information Theory and Coding*. New York: McGraw-Hill.

Anderson, R. G. 1978. *Data Processing and Management Information Systems,* 2nd edition. London: MacDonald and Evans Ltd.

ANSI/X3/SPARC Study Group. 1978. The ANSI/X3/SPARC DBMS framework, report of the study group on database management systems, D. Tsichritzis and A. Klug (editors), *Information Systems*, *3*, 3, pp. 173–91.

Astrahan, M. M. *et al.* 1976. System R – A Relational Approach to Database Management, *ACM Transactions on Database Systems*, *1*, 2, pp. 97–137.

Astrahan, M. M. *et al.* 1979. System R: An architectural update, IBM Research Report RJ 2581.

Bachman, C. W. and Daya, M. 1978. The Role Concept in Data Models, *Proc. 3rd International Conference on Very Large Data Bases*, Tokyo, pp. 464–76 and Infotech State of the Art Tutorial on Advances in Database Technology, London.

Bayer, R. and McCreight, C. 1972. Organization and maintenance of large ordered indices, *Acta Informatica*, *1*, 3, pp. 173–89 and *Proc. ACM SIGFIDET Workshop on Data Description and Access*, Houston, Texas, Nov. 1970.

Bhaskar, K. N. 1978. *Building Financial Models: A Simulation Approach*. London: Associated Business Press.

Bingham, J. E. and Davies, G. W. P. 1971. *A Handbook of Systems Analysis*. London: Macmillan.

Bodnar, G. H. 1980. *Accounting Information Systems*. Mass: Allyn and Bacon Inc.

Borkin, S. A. 1980. The Semantic Relation Model: foundation for a user interface, *Proc. 1st International Conference on Database*, Aberdeen, pp. 47–64. London: Heyden/BCS.

Chen, P. P–S. 1976. The Entity-Relational Model: Towards a Unified View of Data, *ACM Transactions of Database Systems*, *1*, 1, pp. 9–36.

Clifton, H. D. 1978. *Business Data Systems*. London: Prentice-Hall.

CODASYL. 1971. *Database Task Group Report*. New York: ACM and London: BCS.

Codd, E. F. 1970. A Relational Model of Data for Large Shared Data Banks, *Communications of ACM*, *13*, 6, pp. 377–87.

Colton, K. W. and Kraemer, K. L. 1980. *Computers and Banking – Electronic Funds Transfer Systems and Public Policy*. New York; Plenum Press.

Comer, D. 1979. The Ubiquitous B-tree, *ACM Computing Surveys*, *11*, 2, pp. 121–37.

Cushing, B. E. 1978. *Accounting, Information Systems and Business Organisation*. Reading, Mass: Addison-Wesley Inc.

Date, C. J. 1977. *An Introduction to Database Systems*, 3rd edition. Reading, Mass: Addison-Wesley Inc.

Davis, G. B. 1974. *Management Information Systems: Conceptual Foundations, Structure, and Development*. Kogakusha: McGraw-Hill Inc.

Deen, S. M. 1977. *Fundamentals of Data Base Systems*. London: Macmillan.

Deen, S. M. 1981. The state of the art in database research. Aberdeen University Technical Report AUCS/TR-8102.

Edwards, B. J. 1977. Choice of block sizes for magnetic tape files, *The Computer Journal*, *20*, 1, pp. 10–14.

Fagin, R. 1977. Multivalued Dependencies and a New Normal Form for Relational Databases, *ACM Transactions on Database Systems*, *2*, 3, pp. 262–78.

Gottlieb, C. C. and Gottlieb, L. R. 1978. *Data Types and Structures*. Englewood Cliffs, N. J: Prentice-Hall.

Hansen, O. 1977. File design, Part II: Update handling, *Computer Weekly*, September 8, p. 8.

Hicks, J. O. and Leininger, W. E. 1981. *Accounting Information Systems*. St Paul, Minnesota: West.

Jackson, M. A. 1975. *Principles of Program Design*. London: Academic Press.

Jenkins, B. and Pinkney, A. 1979. *An Audit Approach to Computers: A New Practice Manual.* London: Institute of Chartered Accountants in England and Wales.

King, P. J. H. 1966. Conversion of Decision Tables to Computer Programs by Rule Mask Techniques, *Communications of ACM, 9*, 11, pp. 796–801.

King, P. J. H. 1967. Decision tables, *The Computer Journal, 10*, 2, pp. 135–42.

Knuth, D. E. 1973. *The Art of Computer Programming*, Vol. 3: Sorting and Searching. Reading, Mass: Addison-Wesley Inc.

Lee, B. 1978. *Introducing Systems Analysis and Design*, Vol. 1. Manchester: NCC Publications.

Lister, A. M. 1975. *Fundamentals of Operating Systems.* London: Macmillan.

Martin, J. 1967. *Design of Real Time Computer Systems.* Englewood Cliffs, N. J.: Prentice-Hall, Inc.

Martin, J. 1973a. *Design of Man-computer Dialogues.* Englewood Cliffs, N. J.: Prentice-Hall Inc.

Martin, J. 1973b. *Security, Accuracy and Privacy in Computer Systems.* Englewood Cliffs, N. J.: Prentice-Hall Inc.

Murdick, R. G., Fuller, T. C., Ross, J. E., and Winermark, F. J. 1978. *Accounting Information Systems.* Englewood Cliffs, N. J.: Prentice-Hall Inc.

Oliver, E. C. and Chapman, R. J. 1979. *Data Processing, An Instructional Manual for Business and Accountancy Students*, 4th edition. Winchester, Hants: DP Publications.

Page, E. S. and Wilson, L. B. 1978. *Information Representation and Manipulation in a Computer*, 2nd edition. Cambridge: Cambridge University Press.

Page, J. and Hooper, P. 1979. *Accounting and Information Systems.* Virginia: Reston Publishing Company, Inc.

Palmer, I. R. 1978. Practicalities in applying formal methodology in data analysis, *Proc. New York University Symposium on Database Design* and *Proc. BCS Conference on Data Analysis for Information Systems Design.*

Pritchard, J. A. T. 1976. *An Introduction to On-Line Systems*, 2nd edition. Manchester: NCC Publications.

Ries, D. R. and Stonebraker, M. 1977. Effects of Locking Granularity in a Database Management System, *ACM Transactions on Database Systems, 2, 3, pp. 233–46.*

Sanders, D. H. 1979. *Computers in Business: An Introduction.* New York: McGraw-Hill.

Shave, M. J. R. 1975. *Data Structures.* Maidenhead: McGraw-Hill.

Shave, M. J. R. 1980. Problems of integrity and distributed databases, *Software-Practice and Experience, 10*, pp. 135–47.

Shave, M. J. R. 1981. Entities, functions and binary relations: steps to a conceptual schema, *The Computer Journal, 24*, 1, pp. 42–7.

Smillie, K. W. and Shave, M. J. R. 1975. Converting decision tables to computer programs, *The Computer Journal, 18*, 2, pp. 108–11.

Teory, T. J. and Fry, J. P. 1980. The logical record access approach to database design, *ACM Computing Surveys, 12*, 2, pp. 179–211.

Waters, S. J. 1971. Blocking sequentially processed magnetic files, *The Computer Journal, 14*, 2, pp. 109–12.

Index

interrupt, 2, 14, 157
inverted file, 126, 127–31, 135
invoice, 34, 232

Jenkins B. and Pinkney A., 212
journal, 50, 51

key, 59, 98, 126, 135, 193
key-to-store, 83–5
Kimball tag, 88
King P. J. H., 102
Knuth D. E., 65, 135

latency, 18, 22
leased line, 160
ledger, 35, 45, 50–2, 54, 118
liability, *see* claim
library routine, 11, 14
line organisation, 28
link record, 187
linked storage, 133
loan capital, *see* debenture
local overflow, 73
logical data base, 190
logical record, 20, 59, 75

magnetic ink character recognition (MICR), 86
mainframe system, 15
Martin J., 166, 221
member, 180, 186
memory,
    auxiliary, 17–23
    random access (RAM), 15, 156
    read only (ROM), 15
menu, 168
merge, 60, 61, 138, 144
    balanced, 139
    polyphase, 140
microcomputer system, 15
microprocessor, 15
mid-square method, 64
minicomputer system, 15
model,
    econometric, 236, 238
    entity, 181, 184
    financial (corporate), 235
    functional, 183
    logical data base, 179, 185
modem, 157
modulation, 157
multiaccess, 12
multidrop formation, 160
multilevel index, 68, 70, 72, 147
multilist file, 126, 131–5
multiplexing, 157, 160
multiprogramming, 12, 76, 157

network data base system, 186–9, 193
noise, 99, 160
nominal ledger, 35

normal form, 196, 197
normalisation, 195

object code, 11
on-line system, 13, 73, 166–71, 221, 222
on-line terminal, 2, 83, 157
one-to-one (1, 1) transformation, 62, 66
operating system, 7, 10–14
optical character recognition (OCR), 88
optical mark recognition (OMR), 86
optimal solution, 6
organisation,
    business, 27–32
    file, 22, 59–75, 126
    functional, 28
    line, 28
overflow, 65, 66, 70–3
owner, 180, 186

PTT, 159
package, 15
packing density, 22, 73
Page E. S. and Wilson L. B., 92, 135
Palmer I. R., 180
parallel running, 8
parent-child relationship, 189
partial index, 68
partition, 12
physical data base, 189
physical record, *see* block
pilot running, 8
point-of-sale terminal, 88
polyphase merge, 140
posting, 50
prime (primary) index, 130
primary processing sequence, 190, 192
prime (primary) key, 59, 127
privacy lock, 211
procedures manual, 54
profit and loss account, 25, 40, 42–4, 48, 49
progressive linear overflow, 65
punched card, 85
punched paper tape, 85
purchase ledger, 35, 51

quadratic overflow, 65
quicksort, 137

random access, 22, 62
random access file, 62–7
random access index, 68
random access memory (RAM), 15, 156
read only memory (ROM), 15
real-time, 2, 13, 162–74, 232–5
record,
    variable length, 76
    also see logical record
record format, 75–6
recovery procedure, 202
relation, 193
relational algebra, 194

relational calculus, 194
relational data base, 193–7
relationship, 180, 187, 188
  degree of, 180
  parent-child, 189
reliability, 167
remote job entry, 13
repetition error, 91
reservation system, 167, 171
residue function, 64
response time, 166
responsibility accounting, 32
retained earnings, 41
risk analysis, 92, 212
rule mask method, *see* decision table
run diagram, 118

SQL, 194
sales ledger, 35, 51
Sanders D. H., 165
schema, 178, 188
secondary index, 127, 130, 131–3, 192
secondary key, 60, 127
sector, of a disk, 18, 20
security, 200, 211
seek area, 18, 70, 73
seek time, 18, 22, 78
segment, 189
sequential access, 22, 60, 68, 73
sequential file, 60–2
serial access, 22, 59
serial file, 59
set, 186
shareholder, 37, 41
Shave M. J. R., 180
simplex circuit, 159
simulation, 218, 235
skip sequential access, 78
Smillie K. W. and Shave M. J. R., 104
software, 7, 14
sorting, 60, 126, 135–51
  detached keys, 145
source code, 11
sources and application of funds statement, 25, 44, 49
spooling, 12
star formation, 160
storage, *see* memory

subschema, 189
subsidiary ledger, 51, 208
substantive tests, 210, 213, 219
system analyst, 2, 5, 7, 10, 34
system design, 4, 5, 82, 208
system flowchart, 107

T-account, 50
tagged overflow, 71
tape (magnetic), 22–3, 60, 74, 76–8
  interblock gap, 22, 77
  packing density, 22, 73
tape (punched paper), 85
Telenet, 160
terminal,
  hard copy, 12, 82
  on-line, 2, 83, 157
  video, 12, 82
test data, 8
time series analysis, 237
time slice, 12
timesharing, 12, 164
tournament sort, 142
trade investment, 41
transaction, 2, 24, 32, 202, 209
transaction log, 157, 202, 217
transcription error, 91
transfer (transmission) time, 18, 78
transitive dependence, 197
transmission, 159
transparency, 5
transposition error, 91
tree sort, 145
  B-tree, 70, 147–51
tree structure, 70, 145, 147
trial balance, 70
tuple, 193
turnkey system, 15

VSAM, 71–2
validation, 83, 89–92, 210
variable length record, 76
verification, 84, 89, 210
video terminal, 12, 82
volatility, 58, 73, 74

Waters S. J., 78
word-processing, 234